byob

Build Your Own Business
IN 30 DAYS

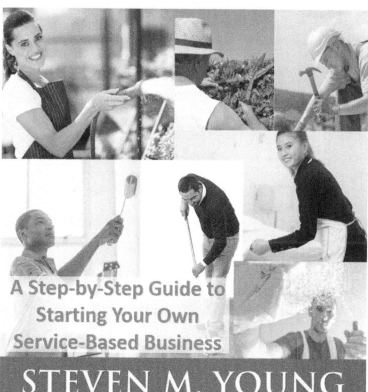

A Step-by-Step Guide to
Starting Your Own
Service-Based Business

STEVEN M. YOUNG

First Printing, 2017 – BLACK & WHITE VERSION

ISBN-13: 978-1974469079
ISBN-10: 1974469077

Cover design: Shamim Rashid

 Published by: YesBear Publishing
3260 E. Lake Drive
Nashville TN 37214

  www.facebook.com/BYOBin30days

  www.BYOBin30days.com

Author available for speaking and coaching

CONTACT INFO:
Steve Young with *BYOB in 30 Days*
steve@BYOBin30days.com

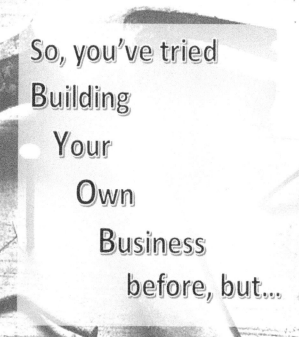

So, you've tried
Building
Your
Own
Business
before, but...

Get your FREE Checklist at
BYOBin30days.com/checklist

TABLE OF CONTENTS

Forward by Philip Rykwalder   6

My Story & Why I Wrote This Book   7

BYOB: Build Your Own Business in 30 Days

Week One: Foundation Phase   14
Week Two: Setup Phase   31
Week Three: Business Phase   40
Week Four: Marketing Phase   59
Winning Attitudes for Business   66

Bonus Chapters – Extra Credit!

Getting Your First Clients   73
Money   78
Advertising   89
Internet   98
Clients   105
Supplies & Equipment   124
Employees I – Hiring   132
Employees II – Managing & Firing   148
Business   174
Example Proposal   192
BYOB Checklist to Check Off!   194
Index   198

FORWARD

I am thrilled to be writing the foreword to this book. I had the privilege of selling Steve his first business in 2012, Renew Mobile Detailing. In three short years, he tripled the business and now runs it efficiently working only about 10 hours a week.

After watching Steve succeed with Renew I have also seen him start, operate and lead other businesses. His ability to understand and meet the market's needs in profitable ways are among the strongest of all the business people I know. Steve has the unique ability to close deals and make clients feel like they are the winner in the exchange. Beyond that, Steve understands the value employees serve in his organizations and he treats them well.

What you'll find in this book are all the nuts and bolts of business. Whether it is a Fortune 500 business or a mom and pop commerce, the marketing, accounting, and systems may not seem like initial needs, but they are crucial to a company's success. This book provides you with a solid beginning of the skills you'll need to Build Your Own Business.

At age 49, Steve reinvented himself in what was likely a scary and exciting time –perhaps you're in a similar space. My hope for you, the reader, is that you will take these valuable lessons to heart. You'll find no fluff or unnecessary instruction here. Know this – following the guidance in this book will set you up for a profitable and successful business.

Philip Rykwalder,
Real Estate Investor
Nashville, Tennessee

BUILD YOUR OWN BUSINESS
IN 30 DAYS

MY STORY AND WHY I WROTE THIS BOOK

BUYING THE BUSINESS

My vocation for most of my adult life was in Christian ministry. I was a paid staff member in either a church or some other Christian organization. When we moved to Nashville several years ago, we had to reinvent ourselves. My father had been a "serial entrepreneur" before people used that word, and I guess the desire to run businesses is in my DNA!

When I bought my service business (*Renew Mobile Detailing*) in 2012, I had never run a business before. I had to learn all these "businessy" things from scratch. I must have done well, because my business has tripled in five years!

SON-IN-LAW'S QUESTION

I hired my daughter's husband (then he was only her boyfriend!) to work as an employee. As he's grown with the business, I've given more and more responsibility to him. A few months ago, he spoke to me about the possibility of buying the business from me some day. He said, "I know how to detail cars, train new workers, and deal with clients, but I don't know about the business side of things."

I began to write out what I'd learned since beginning the business. As I wrote these wonderful little nuggets of wisdom for my son-in-law, I thought these same ideas could help others start their own service businesses. I hope you think so too!

First, let me address another question: "What is a Service Business?"

SERVICE AS A BUSINESS

A service business provides a service that the client may be able to do themselves, but they don't want to expend the time or energy to do it. Certainly, a professional could do it with better quality, but if they had to, the client could do it themselves. *A service business does not offer a physical product; it takes the item already owned by the client and makes it better.* The client owns a lawn before and after the lawn service provider does his thing, but it looks much better after the service is performed.

Certainly, any business will benefit from some of the ideas in this book, but as I've written the book, I've focused primarily on business owners in the service industry.

Here are some examples of Service Businesses.

- Car detailing
- Car repair
- Chimney sweep
- Clothing repair & alterations
- Concrete sealing
- Cutting or styling hair
- Furniture repair
- Gutter installation & cleaning
- House cleaning
- Lawn care
- Manicure/pedicure
- Masonry/stonework
- Oil change
- Painting
- Piano tuning
- Plumbing
- Power-washing
- Re-upholstering furniture
- Roofing
- Any type of repair work
- Any type of cleaning work

This is just a partial list. You may have some additional suggestions, and I would welcome them at steve@BOYBin30days.com. But you can use this list as an idea prompter for your own service business. (See *Foundation Phase*, p. 14.)

Right here at the beginning of our discussion about your business, I've provided for you a concise step-by-step guide for **B**uilding **Y**our **O**wn **B**usiness in the next 30 days. You'll see that I've addressed each of these steps in the first section of the book (pages 14-68). Just complete these items and you can start your business in the next month!

Then, you'll find many more elements for a successful business contained in the Bonus Chapters in the second section of the book (pages 73-192). Here at the beginning, I recommend you read only those pages needed to begin. You can read the others after the next month or if you have some extra time to plan for the future growth of your business.

NOTE: I have put this checklist in the back of the book again, so you can use it as a tool to help you march toward your goal. I recommend printing it out and filling in the dates for each week, using it as a prompt for marching through each of the phases of your business startup. Enjoy!

WEEK ONE: FOUNDATION PHASE

- Determine the service your business will provide. (p. 14)
- Check out competing services in your area. (p. 15)
- Write out the foundational values you will have for your business. (p. 17)

- Decide on the name for your business. (p. 22)
- Determine your scope of services—what is included or not. (p. 23)
- Design your perfect client, or your "avatar." (p. 25)
- Determine the prices you will charge for each service. (p. 26)

WEEK TWO: SETUP PHASE

- List the basic materials you need to begin – tools & supplies. (p. 31)
- Buy the tools & supplies you are lacking. (p. 32)
- Decide on an accounting system for your business (paper or online), purchase it, and enter all expenses thus far. (p. 33)
- Set up business phone number and business email account. (p. 34)
- Design "pitch scripts" in 1-minute, 5-minutes, and 10-minute formats. (p. 36)
- Design phone "script" for answering and/or returning calls. (p. 37)

WEEK THREE: BUSINESS PHASE

- Get your business license and Federal Employer Identification Number (FEIN). (p. 41)
- Set up government accounts with your state or county – Sales Tax, Labor, etc. (p. 44)

- Open a business bank account, or accounts. (p. 46)
- Set up account with credit card processor, if accepting credit/debit cards. (p. 48)
- Set up Facebook account for your business and other free online locations. (p. 51)
- Print business cards. (p. 52)
- Get insurance for your business (recommended, but optional). (p. 55)

WEEK FOUR: MARKETING PHASE

- Begin "spreading the word" about your new business at least one week before beginning to accept clients. (p. 59)
- Do some "freebies" or deeply discounted services for friends & family for reviews or references. (p. 59)
- Attend local networking meetings to tell about your new business. (p. 60)
- Purchase the website domain for your business. (p. 60)
- Set up a simple website. (p. 62)

Week One
Foundation Phase

Before beginning any building, the unseen work of the foundation must be completed. If this doesn't happen, the building will never stand the test of time. The same goes for **B**uilding **Y**our **O**wn **B**usiness—invest the time and effort in the foundation and the business could last a lifetime!

1. Determine the Service Your Business Will Provide

Here at the beginning, you'll want to nail down just what type of service business you want to start. Perhaps you've already decided, so you can skip this section and begin the next section in this chapter. If you haven't nailed down your service area, let me help you think through some ideas.

Read through this section, then get a piece of paper and answer these questions in writing. There is something powerful in putting pen to paper and seeing your thoughts written out before you.

- What are you good at doing?
- What interests do you have?

- What experiences have you had in the past performing service-type work (not necessarily for pay)?
- When your family and friends come to you asking for help, what do they ask you to do?
- Look through the list of possible service businesses (p. 9), see which ones are possibilities, and write them down. Write down any other service that comes to mind as you read this list.

You'll want to decide on some service area where you don't have to have a lot of training to complete. If you can choose something you could start tomorrow, that would be better than something that requires 6 months of training.

NOTE: If, however, you're not desperate to begin working as soon as possible, a long-term possibility could be a service area that requires some training. As a rule, the more difficult the service task, the less competition there will be in that area. If you are in a position to spend 6 months on training, you will be ahead of those who can't spend that kind of time!

2. Check Out Competing Services in Your Area

Once you've decided on a type of service business, look in your local area at those who are already offering that service. You want to find out if there is a market of people willing to pay for the type of service you want to offer. Pretend you are a future client and you are looking online for someone to provide your particular service. Determine how many businesses are out there currently, how big they are, what specific services they offer and what these services cost the client.

Just because there are a lot of the same businesses in the same service field does not necessarily mean you shouldn't start your own. It just means there are many clients looking for this type of service. That's a good thing!

As you look at all these "competitors," be thinking how you can set yourself apart from them. What services do they not offer that you could offer? What services do they offer that you could improve upon?

Try this trick: look at the reviews of these other businesses on sites like Yelp. See what former clients are saying about them. What complaints do they have? What if you offered a business that strove to eliminate this complaint?

For example, maybe one of the big complaints of a business was that they were always late. You could build a business saying, "We'll be on time or your order is discounted by 10%!"

Maybe they say the associate with the other business was rude and disrespectful. Your advertising tagline could be "We're the respectful window washers!"

Be sure to study what these other companies charge for their services. If you charged the same, could you make a profit? If not, this may mean you'll have to offer a higher quality service to get a higher fee for the work!

For extra information about this subject, check out the Bonus Chapter, *Competition* on page 128.

3. Write Out the Foundational Values You Will Have For Your Business

Before you even begin your business, it's best to determine just how you'll behave as a business owner. Values, scruples, rules— whatever you want to call them—they need to be decided before you are in a position to have to decide under pressure. The ideas below are not an exhaustive list, but they will get you going in the right direction. Spend time imagining your first client to see what other "hows" you need to determine beforehand.

HONESTY

You've heard it said, "Honesty is the best policy." I'd advocate for that too! If you're honest with everyone, you don't have to remember what you said to whom. Your lies will always find you out, and once you've lost trust, it's very hard to get back. If you've lost it with a client, they'll never come back, and they could hurt you with bad reviews.

If you lose it with your employees, they will have less motivation to be upright with you. You'll have to be more diligent in watching for employee theft and equipment abuse.

17

If you're dishonest with finances, you could get into legal trouble. Not reporting income will get in you a lot of hot water with Uncle Sam.

Personally, dishonesty is one of the quickest way to get fired from my company. If an employee lies or steals from me or my clients, he's out! If I must second-guess every conversation or check up on him with clients trying to catch the next lie, it's just not worth the effort. I'd rather hire a replacement who will be honest.

DEBT

Most debt can be avoided altogether by planning ahead. Anticipating seasonal shortfalls and watching for upcoming regular outgoing payments will keep you out of a lot of debt complications!

Taking on debt in the beginning of a business venture is a risky proposition. With any kind of debt, you are presuming on certain results occurring in the future. You are given money today, promising that you'll pay it back (with interest) sometime in the future. You're assuming that you will have more money in the future than you have now. You might be saying sarcastically, "Duh, Steve! Like I didn't know that!" but I wanted to make it clear for you here.

If, however, you are able to buy all your equipment and supplies in the beginning with cash, you don't have that added debt pressure to perform above and beyond your regular monthly needs. And if (God forbid) the business goes south, you already own your equipment and can sell it yourself.

Except for the obligation to my monthly note to the previous owner to buy the business, I've run my business without any formal debt (with some of the exceptions noted below). It has been freeing to know that the only thing I had to pay was that note. The rest of my revenue could go toward the profit of my business.

Some advisors may want to help you "leverage your debt" or use other debt strategies, but the no-debt way has worked well for me. However, here are some other forms of debt to be careful of.

- **Beginning capital** – There are many companies and some individuals who would like to loan you money to begin your business. They do this for a portion of the ownership of your company or with a well laid out plan to pay them back.
- **Credit cards** – Banks want you to have a business credit card. They say it will help to "establish your credit" for future loans. If you plan to not borrow money, this feature has no merit for you. Some cards come with features like 5% cash back, air miles, or some other perks. "Charge everything on the card and then pay the balance at the end of the month," they say, knowing 99.99% of the population never does this. Beware!
- **Long-term contracts** – This is the debt category that snuck up on me. I've made several agreements for advertising that locked me into a 12-month contract that may have been good in

the opening months, but sucked me dry during the slow months. These types of contracts may be necessary but keep in mind that you still have to pay the fee during those lean months.

However you decide to run your business with regard to taking on debt, just be sure the debt doesn't pressure you to make bad decisions. If you will stay true to the foundational business principles, you'll eventually make money to pay back the debts if they're not too great.

COMPETITION

In all likelihood, you will not be the only business in your field. Others will have started before you and others will begin after you begin. How are you going to interact with your competition, speak about them, and distinguish yourself from them?

- **Best buds—NOT!** Since you and your competition are vying for the same clients, you're probably not gonna be the best of pals. This is fine; there are other people available to fill that relationship need. But it would be to your advantage to be cordial with them.

- **Speak well of them.** I have had the opportunity to send business to my competition when we were overbooked. They have, in turn, sent some clients to us. This promotes goodwill between us, but also causes our clients to be pleasantly surprised. We actually win loyalty by referring to the "other guy" because the client feels we are more concerned about getting their needs met than earning a buck. Now, you want to make sure the competition is honest and they do a good job before you recommend them, or their bad reputation will spill over on you.

- **Be a cut above.** Being the best you can be with quality work, client care, and consistency will go a long way toward distinguishing you from your competition. Our market area is car detailing. There are many "businesses" that pop up in the summer that are gone by the end of the summer. The fact that my business has been up and running for over seven years is impressive for my clients. They trust me more because I've been here a long time and I'm not going away!

- **Have an abundance attitude!** We will discuss this later in the book in the section about *Winning Attitudes in Business* (p. 66). The boiled-down sense of this principle is realizing that there is plenty of business out there for everyone. In my business, I know there are plenty of dirty cars out there and somebody's got to clean them! Recognize that some clients will call you, and some clients will call your competition. Just make sure you do a fantastic job with your clients, and they won't leave to go to the competition.

4. Decide on the Name for Your Business

Deciding on the name for your business can be a fun process, but there are several things to consider. If you have to explain your name or apologize for it, that's not a good sign!

- **Consider the emotional impact of your name on the client.** Your business name is most likely the first impression you'll make on your future clients. You want a name that gives them a good feeling about hiring you. I have a friend whose business is named *Happy Client Cleaning Service*. I know when I use her service, she wants me to be happy!

- **Don't use puns that only you understand.** Inside jokes and puns are always dangerous to use, unless they are so terrible, everyone remembers it. Recently, I saw a couple of businesses named *Unbeweaveable Hair Supply* and also *Curl Up & Dye Family Hair Care*.

- **Consider the long-term significance of using your own name.** What if your business becomes wildly successful and one day you want to sell it? A name like *John Smith Lawn Care* will be difficult to sell if John Smith isn't around anymore.

- **Don't use "inc" in your name unless your business is actually incorporated.** This caution is pretty straightforward. In most states, it's considered fraud to use "inc" if you're not incorporated. Even if you have a LLC, this is still not an incorporated business. (see *Types of Businesses*, p. 40.)

- **Consider a name that will work well with your website later.** Your website name may not actually be the name of your business, but it could be. It's good to think about this during this phase because it does have a bearing on what you want your business name to be. (See *Set Up a Simple Website*, p. 62.)

- **Check local & state registries to see that your name is available.** Since you'll want to register your business name with the state and federal registries, check first to see if the name is taken. The Secretary of State website for your state should have a searchable database for this step. You should also do a Google search for your potential business name or similar names.

NOTE: You can also have a "parent" company and a DBA—"Doing Business As" business name. For instance, my company is *Young Enterprises LLC* with a DBA of *Renew* Mobile Detailing. (See *Doing Business As*, p. 42)

---

5. Determine Your Scope of Services

You need to think through what your business will do and what it will *not* do. What is included your service and what is not?

Deciding this in the beginning will help in several ways.

- **You can say "no" to those jobs that are outside your scope.** If you get a call from a client who asks to do something you determined is outside of your scope of services, it's easier to say "no" to them. Ask if it's a deal breaker, or would they consider you doing what you can and leaving the other for another business to complete. You may still get the job!

- **It will show you how to market your business.** If you know what you're offering and what you're not offering, this information will help you know who to target in your marketing. You can focus your marketing activity seeking those clients who need the exact services you can provide!

- **You will determine what equipment is needed or not needed.** Once your list of offered services is complete, you will have all the information you need to build a needed equipment list (see *List the Basic Materials You Need to Begin*, p. 31). You'll also have a list of items you *won't* need. For instance, if you have a window washing service, and you've decided not to service 3rd story windows, you'll know exactly how tall a ladder you'll need.

NOTE: In my detailing business, we don't detail engine compartments nor undercarriages. This is a limiting feature to my business, but it helps me in conversations with my

> clients. If they must have this done, I recommend other businesses to them who may be able to meet their needs. This goodwill I show them causes them to want to use me again in the future.
>
> Additionally, since I know to clean an engine or undercarriage I would need a pressure washer, *not* offering this service allows me to *not* have to buy and maintain this equipment! Double win!

Spend some time writing out a list of the service items you *will* include in your business. Also, be a little creative and imagine those services you may be asked to do; that you know you *cannot* complete for the client. Try to be prepared before you start fielding questions from "live" clients! You will probably add to this list after you begin getting requests from clients.

6. Design Your Perfect Client—Your "Avatar"

It's nice to **B**uild **Y**our **O**wn **B**usiness, but if you can't get any clients, it's not gonna last very long! The first step is to figure out what kind of client you want to attract.

WHAT KIND OF CLIENT DO YOU WANT?

Maybe this is a little weird, but I read an article about urinals in Moscow and Singapore. The management had stuck a small sticker of a fly in the center of the urinal. It was to encourage aiming, and it worked!

Aiming is important! Before you can market your business, you'll need to determine what kind of client you actually want. What type of person would your business appeal to? What are their characteristics and demographics? Try to describe this imaginary person on paper.

How old are they? How much money do they make? What is their living situation? Are they married or single; with kids or without? What challenges do they face? What "pain points" do they have which would cause them to call you? When you know these things, you'll know how to talk with them about how your service will relieve those pain points!

Once you've written a description of your avatar, you can begin marketing with your avatar in mind. You probably won't find a client exactly like your description, but your real clients will be similar and will respond to your advertising. (See also *Who Are Your Clients*, p. 108.)

7. Determine the Prices You Will Charge for Each Service

You'll want to have a healthy tension in beginning a new business between charging too much or charging too little. If you charge too little, your potential clients may think your business is not one of quality, but if you charge too much, you may not get any clients.

Several factors come into play when considering how to set your prices.

- **Time for Money.** There are several advantages to Building Your Own Business, but one is determining for yourself what your time is worth. Basically, you are trading your time for your clients' money. You'll need to determine the minimum amount your time is worth. If you work six hours for a client, and the profit (after expenses & materials) is $60, you're making $10 per hour. You must decide if this amount is enough for you. If it's not, you must charge more.

  This knowledge will help a lot in your dealings with clients. If you're at your minimum profit margin, and a client wants to pay you less, you can turn down the job and look for another client.

- **Enough to Keep Working.** You'll want to make sure you're making enough money to keep doing this service. If you charge so little that you can't work and eat, eventually you'll have to find a way to make more. If month after month, you're not able to make enough to live, you'll have to quit and close your business.

- **When to Raise Prices.** Down the line, you may find that week after week your schedule is so full, you begin losing clients because you can't get to them all. In this case, you really only have three options: you can work more hours (work an extra day a week), hire employees (see *Employees I*, p. 132), or you can go up on your prices.

Going up a bit on what you charge will "weed out" those clients that don't want to pay that much, and thus slow the demand for your service. Problem solved! Certainly, you don't want to slow it down completely, but just enough that you aren't losing clients anymore because of the unavailability in your schedule. Also, since you've just "gotten a raise," it makes working that much more fun!

NOTE: After we started growing my business, we experienced what I described above. Now, we've increased our prices at least twice each year by 5-10%. That's a wonderful growth curve!

An added benefit has been a change in client base. Remember, we're a car detailing business. Because of our price increase, we lost most of those calls on Saturday or Sunday morning saying, "Can you come clean my car? My roommate threw up in it last night!" Now, if we get those calls, we know we're making much more money to complete this service than we had just a few years ago!

Congratulations! You've completed your first week toward **B**uilding **Y**our **O**wn **B**usiness. You could be only three weeks from having everything set and serving your first client.

Go buy yourself a beer or a diet soda and celebrate the work you've done and the days to come! You're on your way!

Week Two
Setup Phase

Now that you've gotten the thinking and theory part of the journey behind you, let's move on to some of the practical tasks for the physical set up of your very own business! Make no mistake, we'll certainly be using our brains some more this week, but for now, we have some specific action points to complete.

Let's get started!

1. List the Basic Materials You Need to Begin

The first thing to be determined is what supplies and equipment you need. Think through each of the services you'll offer in your business. Write down a list of the things you'd need to complete each one.

Examine the list you've come up with. You may already have several items of your own, but there may be some you'll need to buy.

Also, remember that most "household tools" are for use every once in a while, instead of use every day. You may be able to begin your business with the equipment you have at home, but it may need to be replaced more quickly than an "industrial use" version of your equipment. Consider this fact as you think through the tools you lack.

2. Buy the Tools & Supplies You are Lacking

As you begin your business, look for the tools that can get you through *the first few months* of your business. You want to be well-established before you start buying tools with lifetime warranties and such. Buy those tools that can get you through the first season, to build up your business before going deeply into debt just on startup expenses.

Think through the replenishable supplies you'll need also; things like cleaning solutions, or other items you'll use up on each job. Certainly, buying in bulk can save you dollars over time, but again, think about getting enough to set you up for a while as your business is getting its footing before buying a 55-gallon drum of cleaning solution!

I recommend this idea as a rule of thumb: Buy replenishables by the gallon, until it makes sense to buy them by the 5-gallon bucket. Buy tools that will last for

3 months of daily use, until you can buy tools that will last for 2 years or more. (See *Supplies & Equipment*, p. 124 for more information.)

3. Decide on the Accounting System for Your Business, Purchase It, & Enter All Expenses So Far

If you're already familiar with basic business bookkeeping, this shouldn't be too difficult. You'll just need to decide how you want to keep the financial books straight for at least the first 3 months. If you change your mind after that time, it's not a huge deal to change systems and reenter the charges you've had and income you've received.

If you want to go high-tech and use an online system, I recommend QuickBooks. I've used it since the beginning of my business and have been very pleased.

If you want a low-tech solution, go to any office supply store (even Wal-mart will have what you need). Look for a 3-column ledger (even though it looks like there are extra columns for the date and item description.

Use the columns from left to right listing the date, item, income amount, expense amount, and balance of the account.

Apart from your initial deposit to set up the

business, all your other entries will be expenses. You'll use two lines for each entry; the place where you spent the money on the top line, then the items you bought on the second line. Look at the example below.

Date	Item Description	Income	Expense	Balance
6/1	Initial Deposit	500.00		500.00
6/2	Walmart		46.20	453.80
	Broom, mop, bucket, soap			
6/3	Office Depot		8.25	445.55
	Ledger, pens			
6/30	John Client	85.00		530.55
	250 Main Street			

This simple system should get you started. You'll want to read soon the bonus chapter on *Money* (p. 78) to get a comprehensive view of basic accounting and the uses of money in your business.

4. Set Up a Business Phone Number & a Business Email Account

As soon as possible, you'll want to have a phone number and email address that's solely devoted to the business. Mixing personal phone calls and business phone calls sends an unprofessional signal to your clients.

- **Business Phone Number.** I have had a separate cell phone for the "business phone" since beginning my business. This has worked well for me, but it has been a bit cumbersome at times. It means during work hours, I'm carrying two cell phones with me at all times. But this separation of work calls and personal calls, kept me from just answering "Hello?" on the business phone and "This is Steve from Renew Mobile Detailing. How can I help you?" on my personal phone!

Another idea is to set up a virtual phone number with Google Voice. It's free and can be forwarded to any phone you choose. Texts sent to your Google Voice number will be forwarded as well. Clients can leave voicemails on the Google Voice number just like they can on any other phone. This may be another viable option for your new business.

- **Business Email Address.** It's not very professional to have an email address you've used since junior high school. Who wants to hire someone at superduperman87@yahoo.com?

You'll want to have a business email address as well to make sure your personal and business emails aren't getting mixed up. Having all your business emails in one place helps you stay in control of communication with your clients.

If possible, see that your business email is connected to your business website domain name (see *Set Up a Simple Website*, p. 62). For instance, you could have info@myservicebusiness.com as your business email address, where your business domain name is myservicebusiness.com.

If you must at the beginning, you can set up a business email address with a free Google Gmail account. You'll just have to see if your business name is available. Perhaps you could have something like myservicebusiness@gmail.com, where "my service business" is the name of your business.

5. Design a "Pitch Script" in 1-Minute, 5-Minute, and 10-Minute Formats

You'll have several different types of opportunities to talk about your business to potential clients, or those who know your potential clients. To be ready in the moment, you should spend some time developing some "pitches" of different lengths for your business.

- **1-Minute Pitch.** This is your "elevator speech" to answer the passing question, "So, what do you do?" They are not going to sit still for a 20-minute presentation about your business. Figure out (and then write down and memorize) a description of the *benefits* your service provides to your clients. For example, "I own a car detailing business that frees up my clients to keep working or playing while we get sesame seeds out of their instrument panel!" (See *What Your Clients Want*, p. 91 for more info.)

  5-Minute Pitch. This is a bit more in depth and can be a bit more formal. It's for a potential client who has already expressed an interest in hiring you for your service. You will continue to praise the benefits the client will receive, but sprinkle in the specific features and even pricing for the different programs you offer. This is perfect for a networking meeting with several business owners in the same room. (See *Face-to-Face*, p. 89, for more info on business networking.)

- **10-Minute Pitch.** The most formal of all, the 10-minute presentation could incorporate a PowerPoint presentation and even handouts. Still focusing on the benefits to the client, and outlining your services and costs, you will have time here to tell a few stories about satisfied clients and their comments about your work. You may also build in time for questions from the listeners.

> **NOTE**: Be sure that each of these pitches has an appropriate "call to action." You want to put the ball right back in the court of the potential client. You want them to know that you would love for them to be a client, and for them to have zero doubt about the next step to become one!

6. Design a Phone "Script" for Answering and/or Returning Phone Calls

If you take appointments over the phone, you'll want to think through what you'll say to a client in this situation. I would even write it out in the beginning and practice saying it without sounding like you're reading. Even begin a "frequently asked question" section, because you will have many of the same questions from potential clients asked over and over.

The main focus from the beginning of the call is for you to *listen to the client.* You want to be able to *repeat to the client exactly what they need*; and then you'll be able to *tell them exactly why you'll be able to meet that need perfectly*!

Way to go! You're now halfway there to **B**uilding **Y**our **O**wn **B**usiness. Just think what it's gonna be like in the next few weeks as you begin not just spending on setup expenses, but having that income coming in!

Take a break to celebrate what you've accomplished. You've earned it! But then, get right back here as soon as you can to hit it hard with the Week Three projects! Woo hoo!

Week Three
Business Phase

We've tackled some of the practical tasks of setting up your new business; now we do the official stuff! I'm not sure why I think this way, but the tasks for this week make me think, *"Wow, this is really going to happen. There's no going back now!"*

From dealing with the government to the banking industry, we're gonna attack them all! Look out Uncle Sam, here I come!

Types of Businesses

Before you get your business license, you'll need to know what type of business you want to begin. There are several types of businesses depending on several factors, but only two would I recommend for beginning your service business. I'll give a description of each, then you'll need to decide which one is for you.

Sole Proprietorship. This is the most basic type of business. You are the only owner of the business and all its assets, and you alone are responsible for its liabilities. You are personally responsible for your businesses debts. Insurance is a bit higher than an LLC. You can hire employees with a sole proprietorship business. *It does not require a business license.* If you choose, a sole prop, you can skip the next section about getting your business license.

Limited Liability Company (LLC). This type of business offers a layer of protection to you as the owner against legal litigation in case you're sued. While it's more expensive to set up the business legally, insurance is less expensive than a sole proprietorship. It's also easier to receive investment capital to grow your business, and easier to sell it when you would like to. You must carefully maintain separate records for the business and not let your personal money be intermixed.

Personally, I have formed a LLC for my service business because I like the protection for my family. I certainly don't expect the business to go belly up, but if something crazy happened, I feel good that they're not going to be affected.

1. Get Your Business License and Federal Employer Identification Number (FEIN)

There are a few mini-steps to complete today's task. You'll want to think about future expansion and a few other details as you make these decisions.

- **The name on your business license and DBAs.** This may seem a bit confusing but, especially if you may one day have more than one service business, you should choose a more general name on your business license. For instance, your service business may be called *Handy Dan's Handyman Service*, but your business license says, *Daniel Moore Enterprises*

LLC. (For the term "LLC," see the *Types of Businesses*, p. 40.)

With this arrangement, *Daniel Moore Enterprises LLC* would be the legal company name, and *Handy Dan's Handyman Service* would be designated as a **DBA**, or "Doing Business As" (also called a "fictitious business name" or "business alias). You will need to register this DBA with the government offices as well so that you can accept checks made out to *Handy Dan's*. Be sure to show these documents (both the Business License and the DBA document) to your bank, so there will be no problems having checks deposited which are made out to *Handy Dan's.*

Then in the future, when you start your next company—*Moore's Mowing Service*—this too can be a DBA under the same business license. It would look like this:

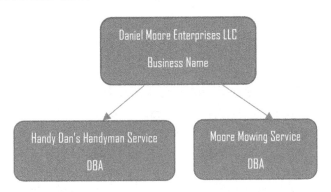

- **Business License.** To do all things above board, you'll need to get a business license (if you're starting a LLC type business). The exact procedure varies a bit from state to state, but it's not as intimidating a procedure as you'd think.

Start by calling the Secretary of State's office in your state and ask where to get your business license. Be sure to ask them if the county, city, and even the municipality where you live requires some sort of formal documentation as well.

- **Federal Employer Identification Number (FEIN).** Again, it may seem intimidating to apply for an official FEDERAL (shudder!) ID number, but it's not really complicated. You can do it online.

Be sure to apply on the official irs.gov site, not the site at www.irs.com which is a paid site made to look like an official government site. There is no cost to get your FIEN; don't be taken by sites that say you must pay.

This official number will be used most assuredly to file your taxes with the government, but also as you deal with other companies who may pay you by check. (See *Filling Out W-9 Forms*, p. 101.)

2. Set Up Government Accounts with Your State or County

"In this world nothing can be said to be certain, except death and taxes!" Benjamin Franklin was a very smart, if a rather pessimistic man! I really can't help with the death part, but here's my stab at getting the taxes part taken care of for your new service business.

[Please know that I am not a legal business expert. I'm just telling you what I've learned to save you some time looking up the information I had to look up. For final answers for your specific business questions in your specific state, please talk with a business professional. Your accountant should be able to answer any question you have.]

- **Sales Tax.** Each state is different in this respect, so you'll need to check out your state, and perhaps your county laws to know what to do with sales taxes. Get online and Google "reporting sales tax [*your* state] to find out which state office you should call first. In Tennessee, the Department of Revenue handles issues like this.

In Tennessee, service businesses like mine are not required to collect sales taxes, so I don't have to worry a lot about it.

The problem with sales taxes is this money is *not your money*. You are collecting a tax from your client for the government, and the government wants you to pass it on to them at regular intervals.

> **CAUTION:** Don't just look at the bottom line of your bank account total and think all that money is yours! Some of it is the government's and they won't like it if you spend it on yourself!

Whether you collect sales taxes or not, you need to report this to the government, usually on a monthly basis. In Tennessee, I report to the *Department of Revenue*. Like I said, Tennessee doesn't require me to charge sales taxes for a service business, but I still have to fill out an online form declaring how much income I had, and how many dollars I charged in sales tax (zero!), and how much I owe the government (zero again!). It feels like a waste of time, but this is how the government wants me to do it, so I do it regularly.

- **Unemployment Insurance Tax (<u>Only</u> If You Have Employees).** Again, each state is different regarding unemployment insurance. The program is set up to ensure that if any of your employees are laid off, they have unemployment insurance available if they qualify.

You'll need to file with the government offices (in Tennessee, it's the *Department of Labor*) on a regular basis. You'll need each employee's name, address, and social security number, as well as the income they're making, usually on a month-to-month basis.

> **NOTE:** Honestly, this was a difficult report for me to keep up with and it was one of the main reasons I went with a payroll company early on. The company files my unemployment insurance paperwork on my behalf. To me, it's worth the money I pay them!

3. **Open a Business Bank Account, or Accounts.** You'll need to go to your bank and set up a business bank account for your business. Take your official state and local documents to verify the name of your business, your DBA designation, and you as the business

owner. Be sure to have your FIEN document (see p. 43) showing this very special number.

When setting up your account, you should keep several things in mind.

- **Try to do business with a bank where you have your personal account already.** Go back to where someone knows you. Try to do most of your transactions at the same branch so they recognize your face. A banker who knows you can be a very special friend when you have banking questions.

- **List your business name, *and* your DBA on your account.** Remember, certainly your official business name should be on your account, but also your DBA name. (See *Get Your Business License*, p. 41.) You will be receiving checks made out to your DBA name, so you don't want any confusion with the bank, like not wanting to deposit your checks!
- **Keep your business and personal accounts separate.** When tax time rolls around, you'll be glad you kept these accounts separate. Make it clear that all income and every expense is business-related.

"Well, how do I get paid, Steve?" I'm glad you asked that question. Set up a regular pay period for yourself; it could be weekly or bi-weekly. Decide what you should get paid, and cut yourself a check every pay period. After three months, evaluate and see if you can get a raise! (See *Owner's Draw*, p. 86) for more information.)

Profit First

I read a book recently called *Profit First* by Mike Michalowicz. I'm still processing it personally and professionally, but I've already implemented a few of his suggestions. His major idea is this:

INCOME − PROFIT = EXPENSES

You'll see this is a little different than the formula I show you in the *Money* section below (p. 78). He determines we should decide what type of profit we want from the business ahead of time, then take that percentage from the income first, and use what's left to cover expenses. His formal argument is based on Parkinson's Law, which supposes we use whatever resources we have to get the job done, no matter the scarcity or abundance of the resources we have to work with.

For instance, if I have 2 weeks or 2 days to get a report completed, I will get the report completed on time. Therefore, if I have $600 to use for expenses or $200, I will make myself meet my expenses no matter what.

With the deposits each day, I'm feeding the total into an excel worksheet which divides the total amount into 5 categories: payroll, profit, taxes, owner's pay, and expenses. I have a percentage for each of them.

With the altered formula above, he is forcing me to work more frugally by limiting my expenses budget to a certain percentage. It's an interesting idea, which I'm still working with. Check back with me periodically at www.BYOBin30days.com/blog for any updates!

You can watch him explain the basic formula on a YouTube video called "Profit First is better for entrepreneurs than 'G.A.A.P.' | Mike Michalowicz | TEDxFultonStreet." Look it up; you'll be glad you did!

4. Set Up an Account with a Credit Card Processor (If You will be Accepting Credit Cards).

Some clients may want to pay by credit card. This is a convenience for them, so they don't have to write a check or carry cash. The advantage to you is that your clients have one more option for paying, and you can set up their recurring payments every month (see Recurring Charges for Clients, p. 82).

To accept credit cards, you'll need an account with a company that does "credit card processing." Your bank can set this up for you or you can sometimes find better rates with other companies. Yes, there is a fee for processing credit cards so you'll have to weigh this in your decision to accept them or not. In my business, the convenience to my clients is enough for me to see the advantage of taking credit cards as a no-brainer!

The fee charged by the credit card processing company depends on the type of card used, and based on a percentage of the amount charged. Visa and MasterCard are usually about the same percentage, while American Express and Discover charge more. In my experience, American Express takes about a day longer than the others for the money to be deposited into my account.

By the way, when you deposit cash into your business account, it is immediately available for you to use. For the checks, it may be 1 to 3 days before the money is available to you. This depends on the bank of origin for the check, and your own bank. Credit card processors usually deposit 2 to 3 days after the charge is initiated.

You have several options for initiating a charge on your client's card.

- *Square*™ – You could have an apparatus like this connected to your smart phone which allows you to physically swipe their card on site.
- **App from Your Credit Card Processing Company** – Many processing companies have an app for your phone where you can punch in the name and numbers for your client's card.

- **Process Manually with Your Home Computer** – The client can just call and give you her information over the phone while you key it into the processing site directly.

- **A Link for Clients to Use with Their Phone or Computer** – Your processing company may provide you with a link to send your client via email or text where they can pay online. I have a similar button on the first page of my website that says "Pay Now" which sends them to the processing company's payment page for my company.

- **The PayPal Option** – PayPal.com also allows you to have a business account through which your clients can pay online. You can email them an invoice and they pay using their phone or computer.

You can explore and use any or all these methods for accepting credit cards.

Important: If you write down the client's information to later enter into your computer manually, be sure to protect that information closely. Destroy this information after its use so that no one else can get it and charge your client for things they didn't buy!

Helpful Hint: The first number of the credit card indicates the type of credit card they're using. A 3- or 4-digit code, which can be on the front or back of the card, is needed for verification also. Sometimes, you'll need the zip code of the billing address as well.

Card Type	Begins with a...	Code digits, where
American Express	3	4 on front
Visa	4	3 on back
MasterCard	5	3 on back
Discover	6	3 on back

5. **Set Up a Facebook Account for Your Business and Use Other Free Online Locations**

You'll want to set up an online presence for your business. Most people searching for your business will do it online first, and most of them from mobile devices!

- **Facebook.** Set up a page specifically devoted to your business. From here you'll be able to post announcements, specials, availability, and advertising for your new business. Friends and family can participate in the growth of your business by sharing your posts with their friends. Be sure to have your contact info and a link to your website. You can start here with directions and the "Create a Page" button: www.facebook.com/business.

- **Google.** Why not have a business listing on the most-used search engine in the world? It's free to set up and it is a repository for good reviews. The more good reviews you get, the higher your ranking with Google. Again, treat this like a mini-website; be sure to have your contact info and a link back to your website. Here's the link to get started: www.google.com/business.

- **Other Free Online Sites.** You'll want to take advantage of several online sites which show your business to their visitors free of charge. Here are a few links to show you some of them:
  Yelp – biz.yelp.com
  Better Business Bureau – bbb.org
  Angie's List – business.angieslist.com

6. Print Business Cards

A good business card will not make or break your business, but it can set you up to win a new client. Keep these things in mind as you plan what goes on your cards.

- **Your First Form of Marketing.** When you hand someone your card, this is the time they have a chance to form a first impression of your business. Take care in designing the card to make sure that first impression is favorable.

- **Be Sure to Have a Byline on Your Card to Affirm a Distinguishing Trait of Your Business.** This could be a major benefit to your client, or the primary intent of your business. For instance, on my business cards for my mobile detailing business, it says, "We Come to YOU!" affirming the mobile aspect of our service. Our clients love the convenience we provide.

- **Take Care in the Design of Your Business Logo.** You'll want an eye-catching logo for those cards you leave in public places waiting to be picked up by you next client. I have used Fiverr.com for several of my logos with great success. On this site, you can get any digital design for as little as $5! I've used them for flyers and other design needs as well.

- **Having a Business Card Establishes a Certain Amount of Professionalism to Your Client.** A "fly-by-night" business, which is here today and gone tomorrow, doesn't take the time to have business cards printed. Having a business card shows your future client that you have invested in your business and take it seriously. This inspires confidence in them.

- **Don't Choose the Cheapest Option When Printing Your Cards.** Paper quality conveys a deeper level of investment in your business. If I receive a card that was printed on a home computer, I wonder if the business owner really thinks his business will be around very long!

- **Don't Forget the Back of Your Card!** A lot of information can be put on the back of your card as well. The back of my card has the pricing for our different packages. This gives the client just that much more information about whether my business will help him or not.

- **What Items Should Be Included on Your Card?**
    Be sure to include these *basics*:
    o Name of the company
    o Contact phone number
    o Contact email address
    o Website address
    o Distinguishing byline (see 2nd point above)
    Additional options you may include:
    o Your name
    o Business address, including city & state
    o Map to your business
    o List of services and/or prices

AN EXAMPLE FROM MY BUSINESS: I have had very good luck having cards printed at *Staples*, by using their online design and ordering feature. I'm able to choose what type of card, where to position my logo and other information, and design the back of the card too. I usually have them sent to the store and I pick them up which saves the shipping charge. It costs somewhere around $20 for 500 cards; less per card if you order more.

7. Get Insurance for Your Business

Insurance is one of those things you purchase that you never want to use! Perhaps you think it's a luxury but as you'll see, it's really a necessity.

- **Your clients will want you to have it.** If you're going into your client's homes or on their property, they'll want to know you have insurance and you'll not be suing them for some injury that may occur. Some businesses you work  in may require seeing your insurance papers before you're allowed to work for them.

- **You will want to have it.** You'll need to be insured in case you or someone you employ damages your client's property. Perhaps you open the car door and it bangs a support pole in the garage and makes a scratch. You'll be glad you're insured rather than pay for these repairs yourself.

- **Insurance adds to your professional status.** When your clients know you're insured, they know you're serious about your business. They want to know they can find you again for future business, and you want them *to want* to find you

- **What kind of insurance do you need?** You'll need to talk with an insurance agent you trust to see what's needed for your type of service business. The insurance should cover at least the client's property. If in the process of your servicing your client's property, you or your employee damages or destroys it, you want to be sure you don't have to sell your business to pay for it! Also, your client will want to be sure you have insurance against employee theft, in case your employee steals something from them.

Note: In the past, I've also had insurance protecting me against theft or damage by my employees of company equipment. I've since discontinued this insurance, mainly because of the quality of my employees. You'll need to make this decision for yourself.

Wow! Look at what you've done! You only have one more week to complete the **B**uilding **Y**our **O**wn **B**usiness process. It's quite an accomplishment. Many people don't get this far. You've demonstrated your own internal dedication and fortitude.

Think of some type of reward you can give yourself. It's important to work, but a key principle is to celebrate your own victories. Maybe it's as simple as eating a favorite dish, or watching that movie you've been wanting to see. Take a short, guilt-less break, then be ready to hit the ground running right at the beginning of the week to sprint toward the finish line!

Week Four
Marketing Phase

You have spent three weeks getting everything in order to have a very successful business, but it can't be successful without clients! You can't benefit your future clients if they don't even know you have this wonderful business. So, let's look at some practical ways to "get the word out" and start serving those clients.

1. **Begin "Spreading the Word" About Your New Business at Least One Week Before Beginning to Accept Clients.**

You want to give yourself a week of preparation before you start accepting new clients. This last week of "marketing" will serve you well once you start "serving" your clients next week. (See *Getting Your First Clients—Step-by-Step*, p. 73.)

2. **Do Some "Freebies" or Deeply Discounted Services for Friends & Family for Reviews & References.**

Some of your friends will let you "practice" on them as test clients. You'll learn a lot from the experience, but also they can put up some reviews online (see *Reviews*, p. 102), or give your some testimonials to put up on your website (see *Set Up a Simple Website*, p. 62).

3. Attend Local Networking Meetings to Tell About Your New Business.

Most communities have a chamber of commerce where local business owners gather to meet each other. Google the phrase "business networking group" and you'll find several groups in your area. When you attend, the key is to learn about the businesses of the *other* attendees. See how you can begin referring business to these other non-competing businesses, and soon they will begin sending you referrals!

Be sure to have your 1-, 5-, and 10-minute pitches prepared for this meeting (see *Pitch Scripts*, p. 36). You'll get plenty of practice at these meetings.

4. Purchase a Business Domain for Your Business.

You may have already investigated a bit about possible domain names when you were deciding on a name for your business (see *Decide on a Name for Your Business*, p. 22). You'll want to determine what to name your website before you start building it. Your company email will also incorporate this domain name (See *Set Up Business Email Account,* p. 34). It needs to be memorable for your future clients. You have several options to consider when determining the name of your website.

- **The name of your business.** For instance, my business website domain name is www.RenewDetailing.com. I've also purchased RenewMobileDetailing.com which just forwards to my main website domain.

- **A description of what you offer.** You may choose not to use your business name for your website. What if you choose something like www.yardofthemonth.com for your lawncare service, or www.makethemshine.com for your window washing service? (These are both taken by the way; sorry!) Try to describe what your service offers, or what benefit the client will receive. Use these brainstorming ideas to decide on your website domain name.

- **If your preferred name is already taken, consider alternate extensions.** For instance, www.yardofthemonth.com is taken, but not www.yardofthemonth.*biz* or www.makethemshine.*net* (these *are* available at the time of this writing)! Check out other possible extensions like .us, or .co, or .pro. These are all good possibilities.

- **Be careful to not get too cute and use plays on words for your site.** I won't put any examples here, but if  you want to see some, just Google "bad domain names." Some may be inappropriate, but I wanted to warn you here first. It would be a lot of trouble to change your domain name if you learned too late it meant something you didn't intend!

You have several options for where to buy your domain name. I've had good luck with www.Godaddy.com for all my domain names. I have been able to set up the business email from this site as well.

5. Set Up a Simple Website.

A simple website is not difficult to set up and is all you really need to get started, but *you do need a website*. Honestly, a small simple website is much better than no website at all. Your website should at least have these components:

- Name of the company
- City and state where you're located
- Services you offer
- Prices or the way pricing is configured
- Contact info – phone number, email address, or a form on the site to message you

Again, you have several options for where you set up your website. I have used WordPress for my website needs. It takes a bit of computer knowledge to set one up, but it's not terribly confusing. You will find a lot of help with YouTube tutorials for any "theme" you choose for your website.

NOTE: Make sure your website is "mobile friendly"—that it looks good when found by a cell phone. Most internet searches today are performed on smart phones rather than home computers or laptops. The screen is smaller (of course!) on a cell phone, so the way your website is displayed on its screen is very different than on a big laptop screen. Most website templates that you modify with your business's information will automatically adjust when accessed by a phone, but you need to make sure before you go to the trouble of building your website completely.

Be sure to check out the bonus chapters below which will help you with marketing your business.

Advertising, p. 89

Internet, p. 98

Congratulations! What an accomplishment for you toward **B**uilding **Y**our **O**wn **B**usiness. Now, you need to keep up the effort to grow your business and keep it as stable as possible.

I've written the basics for you in the above four weeks. Completing these steps has established your business for growth. Certainly, there are other things you can do to enhance your business, so I have included several other topics you can address as bonus chapters following this four-week checklist.

I encourage you to look through the following chapters and read those that apply to you. Make a goal of reading just one chapter each month to see what else you can do to keep your business growing.

WINNING ATTITUDES FOR BUSINESS

Starting and growing your own business is a lot of work for sure! But much of the "work" is not just physical or mental; it's also psychological. Your attitude can make or break your brand-new business. Zig Ziglar has said for years, *"It's your Attitude, not your Aptitude that determines your Altitude!"* Here are three attitudes which will help you reach your greatest potential as a business owner.

AN ABUNDANCE MENTALITY — THERE'S ALWAYS MORE!

You must always remember that there *are* potential clients "out there" who *need* and *want* your services. Your big job is just connecting with them. When you begin to think the pond is drying up and there are no more clients, this attitude will affect how you treat the clients you *do* have. They'll begin to sense the desperate attitude and will want to work with someone else. It will also affect how you treat your competitors. Instead of knowing there's plenty of work for everyone, you'll hoard your clients and begin to talk down your competition. Your clients will hear this in your voice and you'll lose their trust.

If you've done your market research and you've determined there is a market for your service, trust in that and go on as normal. Know that you're going to get your piece of the pie, and so are your competitors. Just connect with *your* clients, and let your competitors connect with *theirs*.

INTEGRITY PAYS BACK – HONESTY IS THE BEST POLICY

The Golden Rule goes like this: "Do unto others as you would have them do unto you." Hold fast to this attitude and you will reap the rewards in your business as well as your life. Being true to your word with everyone will build a trust that cannot be shaken. No one wants to do business with someone they don't trust. When your clients see you follow through on your word even when it no longer makes financial sense, they will know your business is an honest one and will want to use you again and again.

When your employees see you pay them on time and what you agreed to pay them, they will be loyal and faithful to you in the future. What a difference between this type of employee and the one who talks about you behind your back!

Help Others, They'll Help You –
What Goes Around, Comes Around

Another biblical principle says, "You reap what you sow." Several of the laws of the harvest ring true regarding business, including this one. Whatever you plant, you'll get back later. If you plant corn, you won't harvest tomatoes! In business, if you lie to clients, they'll lie to you. If you cheat your employees, they'll cheat you.

Conversely, if you *help* your competitors, they'll help you. I've seen it happen! (See *Competition*, p. 128.) If we don't have an open slot for our client, I refer them to another competing detailing company. After beginning this practice, within a few months, I began to get calls from people who said that my competitor had recommended my business to them for the same reason. This comradery between competing businesses makes the client feel at ease and happy to do business with us both!

A Good Philosophy for Business...

Offer **GOOD SERVICE** TO YOUR **CLIENTS**,

Give **GOOD PAY** TO YOUR **EMPLOYEES**, and

Receive **GOOD PROFIT** AS THE **BUSINESS OWNER!**

Want some additional help BYOBing? Join our BYOB members. You don't have to do this alone!

www.BYOBin30days.com

BONUS CHAPTERS
Extra Credit for You!

Getting Your First Clients   73

Money   78

Advertising   89

Internet   98

Clients   105

Supplies & Equipment   124

Employees I – Hiring   132

Employees II – Managing & Firing   148

Business   174

Example Proposal   192

BYOB Checklist to Check Off!   194

Index   198

GETTING YOUR FIRST CLIENTS
Step-by-Step

Okay, so you've set up your business, but how can you get those first clients? What do you do first? Here we go!

Make a List of First Contacts. Yes, get a piece of paper and start writing down names (or use a computer, but don't get tied up with pretty fonts and organization—it's just a list!). List family and friends who you can call and ask for referrals; people who need your service *now*. Think also of people you know who know a lot of people—your pastor, community leaders, or business people.

Think through different categories of people. For instance, people you grew up with who are still in the area; people you went to school with; people from church or other organizations you participate in. Put all their names on a list, and start getting in touch with them.

Tell them you're "trying to get the word out" about your new service business. Give them the website, offer to get them some business cards, and ask them to think of five people they know who may need services like yours.

Determine Your "Start" Date. It's good to have a target start date to give to people, maybe a week out from when you start calling. I like new things to begin on Mondays, so that's what I'd suggest. If you begin calling people on Monday, the second week of May, tell them you want to fill your schedule beginning Monday, the third week of May. This helps the person you're calling not feel pressured because they know they have several days to "prepare" for your service.

> **NOTE**: If, however, the person on the phone wants to hire you that very day, or some day before your official start date—take it! Never turn down work in the beginning. But when you're not working, be sure you're on the phone connecting with people, especially this first week! I encourage new business owners to "work like they're working." If you were at a "normal" job, you'd be working eight hours a day. So, be sure you're working *at least* eight hours each day to get those first clients!

Start with the Most Likely "Yeses." Begin with those people you're most comfortable with, and give them a call. Talk to them with excitement about your new business, and that you're wanting to start next Monday (or today—like I said above, don't turn down a chance to begin early!). If they are someone you'd like to give a "freebie" for a good review, schedule them as soon as you can. Then, use their review on your website and business Facebook page.

Next, Call the Leaders on Your List. Remember, some of those on your list oversee or have influence over large groups of people. Call these people next. Depending on the relationship you have with them, you could offer a "referral fee" back to them for anyone who comes to you and mentions his name. You might give him a 20% discount for future services, or a small percentage of what the new client pays. It's up to you. But certainly, if you can get a referral without giving away a referral fee, shoot for this first!

Work Your Way Down The List Completely. Yes, even those people who are difficult to talk with, call them all! You may be surprised at the people you're thinking, "They will *never* give me a referral!" might just turn out to be a highly valued client fountain! I tell my kids, "The worst they can say is, 'No, Stupid!' and they probably won't say that!" Don't be afraid of those "scary" people.

Referrals from New Clients. After you have completed your first jobs, get back in touch with your client and ask if she could recommend you to someone else. Tell her that if the friend sets an appointment, you'll give her a discount next time.

BEFORE ASKING FOR A REFERRAL FROM A CLIENT be sure to ask if they liked the service. If they say anything besides, "It was wonderful!" ask them what could have been improved. Be sure to listen for the tone of their voice, not just their words. Explain that you're beginning a new business, and you want to do things very well, and her constructive correction will help you so much. Then...listen carefully. If there's anything you can do immediately to correct the missed areas, do them. If not, explain the next time you'll be sure to pay special attention to those areas. The end goal of this conversation is for your client to know you have her best interests at heart. (See *Complaints*, p. 117.)

MONEY
Get It Right from the Start!

Certainly, getting money is one of the highest motivations for **B**uilding **Y**our **O**wn **B**usiness. You may have heard it said: "It takes money to make money." This is true, and so the basic strategy is pretty simple: *Earn as much money as possible by spending as little money as possible.* That's why you need this chapter. You want to make enough money to pay your expenses and have some left over for yourself. So, here we go— the basics of accounting.

[Also note, I am <u>not</u> an accountant. Do not consider the ideas below as definitive. Please set up your own relationship with a Certified Public Accountant (CPA) to make sure your business is running correctly.]

ACCOUNTING 101

"Accounting" just means keeping up with your money, or *accounting for* where every dollar comes from and where every dollar goes. Your accounting system is your paper (or computer) record of how you follow the money.

For the purpose of this book, let's start with income (although you'll have some expenses before you make a dime. More about that below). On a typical day, you'll provide your service for your client and they will give you a quantity of money for this service. This is your only INCOME. To provide that service, you have to have equipment and supplies which need to have been purchased earlier. These are your EXPENSES. What's left over is your PROFIT.

INCOME – EXPENSES = PROFIT

Not rocket science so far, right? And actually, the simpler the business, the simpler the accounting.

Let's look at it like this. Suppose your business is cleaning houses. The day before your first client, you scrape enough money together to buy a mop, broom, vacuum cleaner (or your borrow your Aunt Bessie's), some Windex, Pledge, and Lysol and enough rags to do the job. Whatever you spend on these supplies and equipment are your EXPENSES. Let's say it comes to $125.

The next day, you go to your client's house, clean it spick and span, and she pays you your fee. Let's assume you make $80. This is your INCOME. Let's see how you did.

$80 (INCOME)

- $125 (EXPENSES)

= -$45 (PROFIT?)

WHAT? Wait, I thought "profit" was supposed to be a positive number? Stay with me; it gets better.

Later that day, you do another house and make another $80. But, even though your income from this client is the same, your expenses are lower. You don't need to buy another mop, broom, or vacuum, or other supplies. Let's say you used all your Pledge in the first house, so you need some more – $5. Let' see how we are now.

$80 (INCOME)

- $5 (EXPENSES)

= $75 (PROFIT!)

Now, that's what I'm talking about! So, combined for the day, you've made $30 profit. Bring that over the whole week, doing 2 houses a day and you've made over $600!

$800 ($80x10 houses, INCOME)

- $175 ($125 + $5/house, EXPENSES)

= $625 (PROFIT!)

These are the basics of simple accounting. Another variable you'll need to consider is those expenses that are not daily, but are monthly, or yearly. Things like insurance and advertising are usually monthly costs, while dues to the *Better Business Bureau* are yearly. You'll also need to determine when you need to buy a new vacuum, or other equipment. You may need to replace it twice a year, and brooms and mops, more often.

To prepare for these future expenses, you should begin at the start of your business to put money aside for those purchases. Maybe you'd like to put it in a special shoebox in your closet, but I'd recommend a separate savings account at your bank called "Future Equipment."

FINANCIAL CATEGORIES FOR YOUR ACCOUNTING

You'll want to keep up with every dollar of expense and every dollar of income. Never mix personal and business expenditures. It will come back to haunt you later! Learn from my mistakes!

Mighty Clean Home Services	
PROFIT & LOSS STATEMENT	
June 2017	
INCOME	
Sales (80x20 clients)	1600
Tips	120
GROSS INCOME	$1720
EXPENSES	
Equipment	125
Supplies	85
Travel ($0.55/mile x 280 miles)	154
TOTAL EXPENSES	$364
NET INCOME	**$1356**

You'll be able to keep up with how you're doing in your business by preparing a report each month called a *Profit & Loss Statement*. I've put one above as an example using the *Accounting 101* (p. 78) ideas.

You may have different income or expense categories but just let this serve as an example. The total of all the sales for your first month is $1600. By the way, in P&L Statements, don't worry about the cents; just round up or down to the nearest dollar.

"Gross" income is not "yucky" income; it just means everything without any expenses calculated yet. It could be that the only type of income you have are "sales." No worries, but you should have several types of expenses.

Don't go crazy here, but break them down enough so that you can look month to month in the future and see where your money is going. You may notice some spike in spending that you can correct in the future. If you're keeping records diligently, you'll know where it's coming from and look for ways to save in future months.

RECURRING CHARGES FOR CLIENTS

Perhaps you have a service that could be performed on a regular basis, say twice per month. You can set up a recurring charge for your client through your credit card processing company. Every period, your client's card will automatically be charged the amount you designate. It's very convenient for the client and very advantageous for you. This system provides a stable financial base you can count on each month.

> **For Example**: In my company, we offer a monthly payment program for our clients. Each month, on a certain day for each client, their monthly payment is charged to their card through our processing company. I don't have to key in anything; money is put into my account automatically! Yee haw—I like that!

RECURRING CHARGES FOR YOU

In the same way, you may subscribe to certain services which will begin to automatically be deducted from your bank account each month. While this is convenient for you, it can mess you up if you don't keep up with which charges are coming out and when. You don't want to be counting on a certain balance only to realize the automatic draft has taken that money from your account the night before.

Incidentally, most of these charges happen at midnight the night before the date you've set up. So, when you wake up the next morning and check your balances, you'll see the charge has been processed. The same timing goes for your client's automatic charges coming to you.

One of the categories you want to have well-covered with its rightful percentage is the taxes category. Because you have **Built Your Own Business** now, Uncle Sam has a "special" tax rate for you. He will want you to estimate what you will owe for the year and send him ¼ of that amount every three months. So, as you're making deposits, determine what percentage you need to hold out to pay these estimated quarterly taxes. This will be another question you want to go over with the accountant you hire for your business.

TAX DEDUCTIBLE EXPENSES

The government knows that to make money you have to spend money. They know that to make your business work, you'll need to spend money on tools, supplies, advertising, gasoline, and several other things. (See *Accounting 101*, p. 78.)

[Be sure to talk with a qualified accountant about these things. I'm writing from my own experience and am not qualified to give accounting advice!]

What does "tax deductible" mean? Think of it this way. Since you could not have made money in your business without expenses, the government allows you to subtract the expenses from what you made, then pay taxes on what's left. For example, say you made $45,000 in sales in your business, but spent $15,000 in expenses. You only have to pay taxes on the $30,000 profit.

Sales	$45,000	
Expenses	- 15,000	
Profit	$30,000	(only pay taxes on this amount!)

Because they won't just take your word about what you've spent, you'll need to keep a clear record and receipts for these expenses. You'll want to eventually put them in categories for your Profit & Loss Statement (See *Accounting 101*, p. 82), and some people may advise you to put these receipts in separate folders as you're going through your year. I have another system; I just put all my receipts throughout the year in a box near my work area. Then, I know where all the receipts are at the end of the year, and I can go through them to file my taxes. Not glamorous, but it's simple and it works!

Here is a partial list of typical expenses that will be tax deductible if you have the proof to back them up:

Advertising
Business Insurance
Car Expenses (a certain percentage)
Home Office Deduction (a certain percentage)*
Meals/Entertainment (eating out on the job)
Office Expenses (printer, ink, paper)
Travel (related to business, keep mileage log)
Other Expenses (training, dues, business magazines)

[*A realtor advised me: "Deducting an amount for a home office can affect your Homestead Exemption break on property taxes. This varies from state to state." Thanks, Mom!]

I'll say this again. *I'm not an accountant, so you must take what I'm saying here for what it is: suggestions from a fellow business owner. I'm not qualified to give legal or accounting advice, so check with your accountant before putting these ideas into practice.* I just want you to be aware of some of the things I was not aware of when I began my business. I'm sure it'll save you a ton of personal headaches!

OWNER'S DRAW

Of course, your employees aren't the only ones who want to be paid every once in a while. You as the owner want some of the cut! In your accounting, you'll call this "Owner's Draw" because you as the owner are drawing out money from your business account for personal use. Be sure to keep up with this figure. It will not show up on your P&L because that statement just demonstrates how profitable the business has been that month. Remember, when you're taking money from the business to pay your own personal bills, it's called the Owner's Draw.

Again, keep in mind any upcoming expenses in the business before taking money for your own personal use. You want to make sure your business is healthy and can continue to run well without the money you're taking out. You don't want to kill the *Goose that Laid the Golden Eggs*! (If you don't know this story, check it out. It's a good life lesson!)

...*But to Begin With*...

Here's a bare basics list of money things to set up before you get your first client.

- **A business bank account (checking)** – At first, all business-related transactions will go in and out of this account. (See the earlier section, *Open a Business Bank Account*, p. 46.)
- **A record-keeping system** – It can be as simple as a paper notebook, or computer software. I have used *QuickBooks* online software for years and it's done everything I've needed to do. (See *Decide on the Accounting System*, p. 33.)
- **Enough money to purchase your first basic equipment and supplies** – You don't have to have the best equipment in the world to begin with; just sufficient for completing the first few months of work. (See *Buy the Tools & Supplies You are Lacking*, p. 32.)

ADVERTISING
Methods of Marketing

How can you, as a new business owner, get the word out that you're ready to work and open for business? Several methods are available to you.

Friends & Family – Talk to friends and family about your services first. Tell them what you've done to get ready to open up shop. Ask if you can provide them with a free or discounted service in exchange for promoting your business. Someone who says, "My nephew's new business came out and washed our windows, and they've never been cleaner!" is a great marketer for your business. Perhaps they could post pictures of your work on Facebook or Instagram, and link back to your website. Also, ask for them to post honest reviews on one of your free sites, like Facebook or Yelp.

Face-to-Face – You will want to begin "networking" with other business owners who are not your competitors. Look online for business networking opportunities. There are several groups who meet weekly to share updates about their businesses, and learn about new businesses. Find these groups and attend with plenty of business cards! Your goal is to get these people to know, like, and trust you over time. Be sure to have your 1- and 5-minute pitches down (see *Pitches,* p. 36) because you'll get a lot of practice at these meetings!

Giveaways – A new business giving away its services for free or a deeply-discounted price can help get those first few clients. These clients in turn can give you referrals to their friends, family, or co-workers who can be "full paying" clients! They, in turn, can post good reviews on your website or others – Better Business Bureau, Angie's List, or Google Business.

Website – I've found most new clients have found our business from an internet search. A good website that provides what a future client is looking for is a wonderful tool for getting new business. Refer to the *What Your Clients Want* section below (p. 89) for what to put on the website. At a bare minimum, it must have a way for the client to contact you, preferably a phone number. Many clients are searching from their cell phones and will want to call to ask questions, rather than search on your website.

Business Facebook Page – Be sure your business has its own Facebook page. You should have pictures of work you've done, contact information, and links back to your website. This page will be sharable by any of your friends, family, or clients. If they share a post from your business Facebook page on their timeline, everyone who visits their timeline will see it. It's good to post something at least weekly on your page so others have the chance to repost it on theirs. (See *Set Up a Facebook Account for Your Business*, p. 51.)

Other Online Methods – You can put up ads on Craigslist which targets potential clients in your local area. Facebook ads allow you to target geographically and by other specific client characteristics. Yelp has some monthly programs which allow for increased exposure on their site.

Be sure these ads point back to your website for contact information. You may want to offer a discount with the mention of the ad; then you can know where the new client lead came from. This information will allow you to increase, decrease, or adjust your marketing efforts on each platform.

What Your Clients Want

Your future clients know that many businesses are not legitimate and they don't want to be taken advantage of, so they are rightfully skeptical of a new business. Your marketing must overcome that skepticism as quickly as possible. Let's think for a moment from the client's point of view. If they are looking for someone to provide a service like yours, what are they looking for in the business they hire?

Well-Established. Future clients want a business that has been around a while and has many satisfied clients because they've proven themselves to many people. This is the one objection you can't overcome *because you're a new business!* But thankfully, there are other things your clients are looking for that you *can* offer. These following suggestions can outweigh this objection so that new clients *will* choose your service business over your competitors!

Professional. Your new clients want to know that the business they're hiring is doing everything right business-wise. You can demonstrate this by offering an adequate range of services,  bringing all your own equipment, and offering invoices or receipts. A good website also promotes the professional image you want to project. Printed products like business cards, flyers, and magnetic signs on your vehicle show them you are a professional who has invested in the business.

Others Like the Business. No one wants to be the "guinea pig" for a new business. They want to know you've done this many times before. I told you earlier just how you might get those *first* clients (see p. 89), but just know this about your client: they don't want to be the "first person to the party!" They are more impressed with "millions served" than "you're my first client!" So, as you are talking to your first clients, emphasize the wonderful benefits of your service, not that you're just starting!

In Their Price Range. Sometimes, price is the driving factor for the client. If your services are not within their price range, you can't do business with them. What you need to do is convince them of your service's *value* before (if possible) talking about prices.

In my car detailing business, I list the services we provide for each package before I tell them the price. I want them to have a complete idea of all the items included in the cost before I hit them with that big number!

WHAT TO PROMOTE IN YOUR MARKETING

The situation for most service businesses is that, honestly, the client could do our service herself if she had to. But for some reason, she'd rather pay us to do it than do it herself. For this, I am thankful! Perhaps she doesn't have time, doesn't want to do it, or knows a professional could do it better than she could.

In your marketing, we need to think about the client and what she is looking for, not what we want to say. We, as business owners, want to talk about all the *features* of our different packages and what we do. The client is thinking (and rightly so) about herself. She is always listening to her favorite radio station—WII-FM, or "**W**hat's **I**n **I**t **F**or **M**e?"

Therefore, in your advertising, focus exclusively on the *benefits to the client*. How will this make the client feel after you're finished? What worries can we alleviate for the client? In advertising, we say, "What *pain points* for the client can we alleviate?" Once you figure this out, you can say things like: "You don't have to worry about

93

a thing. We'll take care of [insert the pain point]!" "Your car will look like new!" "You just keep working or playing, we'll take care of this for you!"

Just remember this little maxim:

Features Tell, but Benefits SELL!

SEASONAL PROMOTIONS

Every month of the year brings special opportunities to promote your business. Those future clients who are on the fence about getting your services just might be pushed over the edge by a special promotion. Take advantage of every one you can.

Be sure to utilize holidays and special dates. Look for opportunities to run specials for Mother's Day, Father's Day, Thanksgiving and Christmas. Don't forget Back-to-School and Beginning-of-Summer specials. Any normal holiday can be a special seasonal promotion!

Take advantage of special seasons related to your business. Think about certain times of the year that have a special significance for your business. For instance, if you have a window washing business, run a Spring Cleaning Special in March and April.

Find (or invent) crazy "national-day-of" days that you can use as an excuse to promote your business. Use this one if you dare! For instance: "Did you drop a dozen donuts on your carpet while celebrating National Donut Day yesterday? Call Carl's Carpet Cleaning service and use this 10% off coupon!"

OTHER FORMS OF MARKETING THAT HAVEN'T WORKED FOR ME

I want you to know as much as I know about marketing, so let me share what I've seen *not work* for my business. Perhaps you'll try them and they'll work for you, but I haven't seen much (any) profit from the following ideas.

Radio Ads. These ads were very expensive and I saw zero return from the effort. I liked the ads themselves, and it was fun to hear them on the air, but they did not result in a single sale!

School Sponsorships. Every once in a while, a school representative will want me to buy an ad in their school paper, or even put my logo on a t-shirt! I haven't seen any return from these efforts. If you are want to support a school in your area, that's great. But don't expect to get clients in return for your investment; just self-satisfaction!

Calendars. These are the same as above. Usually a sports team will have their play schedule set on a wall poster. They sell ads around the border for your business. [I've yet to see these work, but at the time of this writing, I'm trying it one more time to see if it'll work. This time, I'm adding a 10% discount if they mention the ad. I'll let you know on www.BYOBin30days.com if it worked or not!]

Restaurant Tabletop Ads. The salesman on the phone told me that they would have my business on a triangular ad card on each of the tables in a particular restaurant. I saw zero appointments from this type of marketing.

Bathroom Wall Ads (Graffiti). Sounds weird but perhaps you've seen these ads in bathroom stalls. They must work because people keep buying them, but I've seen no return for my business with them.

I've told you about all these ideas not to scare you away from trying to be creative in your advertising, but just to warn you that all things must be weighed. Just because a salesman makes promises doesn't mean it will pan out exactly as he said it would.

A famous Latin phrase says it well: *Caveat emptor* – "Let the buyer beware."

INTERNET
Your Online Presence

Any business which does not have its own website has two strikes against it from the start. Most clients are looking for a new service company through internet searches. Since you want to grow your business as quickly and efficiently as possible, providing an easy way for your future clients to find you on the internet is imperative!

Facebook Business Page. As I've said earlier (p. 51 & 90), a Facebook page dedicated to your business is a good idea. This page is a simple (and free) way to advertise your services to your friends and family first, and then with some help from them, to their friends and family. You can post (with permission) photos of work you've done for your clients in the hopes that the viewers of your Facebook page will want your services as well! Eventually, you may want to have paid advertisements on Facebook too, but the page itself will help greatly when you're just starting out.

Pinterest, Twitter, Instagram, and Other Online Sites. Depending on the type of service business you have, you may want to connect with future clients by engaging in these other online sites too. It seems that generally women frequent Pinterest more than men, so if your business clients are mainly women, Pinterest may be a good place to post photos about your business. Keep your ears open about which online places your clients are frequenting, and see if those sites may be worth considering for your online marketing efforts. Social media can become a "black hole"—all your time gets sucked into it! Be wise and choose just a couple sites to use at first.

Yelp, Google Business, and Other Automatic Sites About Your Business. (See also *Google*, under *Free Online Locations*, p. 52). Some sites make it their business to know about your business. Whenever they find out about a new business, they automatically build a small site about that business. It usually has the basics including name, address, phone number, website, email, and other relevant facts. The primary purpose is for the clients to leave reviews about the business. It's in your best interest to find these "mini-sites" and claim them as your own, so you can (1) make sure the information is correct, and (2) monitor any reviews that are put up about your business. These reviews are very important! (See *Good Reviews*, p. 102)

DANGER: Online marketing and involvement with social media sites can eat up your time! Be sure to manage (and measure) your time on these sites. It's not uncommon to begin "working" on these sites and then look up and four to six hours have gone by! I'd encourage you to set a timer for 30 or 45 minutes and then get offline until the next day. Your time is precious when **B**uilding **Y**our **O**wn **B**usiness; don't waste it playing around on the internet!

EMAIL

Email is a wonderful way to keep in touch with your clients and to help new clients find you in the first place. It is also essential for any new business!

Make sure your email address uses your own website domain name. (See also *Business Email*, p. 35). Having a Gmail or Hotmail email address for your business will only serve to diminish your credibility with future clients. I strongly urge getting a business email connected to your website domain. I have bought all my domains through ww.godaddy.com. You can set up email addresses from this same site. (See also p. 60.)

Build an email list of your clients. With a client list, you can update your clients on upcoming specials or emphases. For instance, at the beginning of March, send an email to clients promoting your "Get Your Yard Ready for Summer" special. Or give them a 10% off coupon they can email to their friends for trying your yard service. Let them know if they do, they get $20 off their next service!

Receive emails from prospective clients. Many times, our first contact with another business is through email. For instance, a car company is participating in a local car show and needs a detailing company to make sure their cars are sparkling! They don't live in my city, so they look on the internet for detailing services in the area. They will either give me a call or often will send an email with their request. Through our email correspondence, I can send them a proposal (see *Example Proposal*, p. 192), and we can agree on a price.

This kind of B2B (Business to Business) client usually has several extra forms to fill out that your private clients will not need to bother with. One is called the W-9 form.

Filling Out W-9 Forms – When engaging in B2B, other businesses may ask you to fill out a W-9 form. Don't act alarmed; just tell them, "Yeah, I'll get that right out to you." Don't worry! The first time I heard the term, I had to look it up on the internet. The W-9 form is a government form your client's company will need for tax purposes. It shows they paid money to another legal entity. You can download the sample form from www.irs.gov. There is no charge for the form. Print it out, fill in all your info, including your Federal Employer Identification Number, or FEIN (see FEIN, p. 43), scan it and email it back to them. No problem!

GOOD REVIEWS

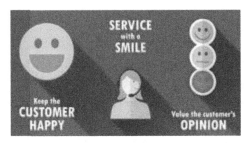

Your client's public reviews of your business can be a great help, or a great hindrance to your business. Monitoring these reviews allows you to minimize bad reviews and capitalize on good ones.

When you get a good review be sure to thank the reviewer as quickly as possible. The review site itself may have a place to respond, so saying thank you in that space allows other review readers to see what a nice person you are. If you can't leave a note directly on the site, give the client a call, email, or send a card thanking them for the review.

When you get a bad review, defending yourself on the site itself rarely is a good idea. If the review is unfounded and has incorrect information, you may want to clarify this for the readers who see it later, but most of the time the "ranting" of a client can be seen for what it is and the reader will dismiss it.

When the bad review is correct, and the discontent of the reviewer is based on bad service on your part, get in touch with him by phone as soon as possible to see if there's anything you can do to "rescue" the client. Offer a partial or full refund, to redo the work, or come again in the future for free. Your goal in talking with the client is to let him know his satisfaction is your highest goal. I use the question, "What can I do to make this right?" It is worth it to me to return all the money, if it will satisfy the client and have him take the review down, or add an update stating what we did to make it right. This helps the reader of the review know we are a company which is very concerned with the satisfaction of our clients.

It's a fact of life that you can't please everyone. If you've done your best and paid attention when a client had some complaints, give yourself a break. Walk away from that client and on to please the next one! You'll learn more about your clients in the next section (see *Clients*, p. 105).

CLIENTS
Ya Gotta Have 'Em!

You're in business to make money. The ones who have the money to make your business work are your clients. I've already written about how to get them (see *Advertising*, p. 89), but now let's talk about how to *keep* them.

"CLIENTS" OR "CUSTOMERS"

While it may not mean that much to some people, the distinction between "client" and "customer" means a lot to me. The term "customer" causes me to look at the person as a dollar sign; they are someone who buys a commodity from me. I see grocery stores and department stores as having customers. There is no relationship; just a buy/sell transaction.

For those of us who are in the service arena, our clients are not just buying something from us like they would from Wal-Mart; they are contracting with us to perform a service for them. Think of an attorney who is hired to represent his client in court. The attorney has a high respect for his client, and the reverse is true as well.

I desire for my clients to feel well-respected and cared-for by my business. I want them to feel the same from my employees. Since both my employees and I treat them with respect, I expect the same from them in return.

For these reasons, I use the term "client" instead of "customer."

WHAT ARE YOU REALLY SELLING TO YOUR CLIENTS?

This question appears obvious on the surface. "I'm selling a house-cleaning service." "I cut their grass." "I clean their cars." Now that we've seen the shallow answers, let's look more closely at the question by asking another one. *"What do your clients really want from you so much that they're willing to pay you money to receive it?"*

Service

This book is written specifically for you, the "service" provider. We're not talking about retail stores or car lots. You provide a physically active service for your clients. Whether is cutting their hair or cutting their lawn, you serve the client. The attitude is this: They don't owe you anything until you've served them. Keep your attitude as the one who is serving the client.

Confidence

Your client is delegating a task to you that (a) she doesn't have time for, (b) she doesn't want to do, or (c) she doesn't have the expertise to do. She wants to give you this job with the confidence that when she returns her attention to it, all her expectations will have been met. In my car detailing business, I tell my clients, "You can keep working or playing while we take care of your car!" They love that feeling of confidence.

Trust

Along with confidence, our clients entrust their property to us for a time. The client expects her property to be returned to her in better condition than when she gave it to us. Whether it's her hair, her nails, or her furniture, she trusts us with it. This trust must be guarded during all phases of our interaction with her. From her first impression at your greeting through to your final ask for payment, be sure her trust only grows and never diminishes.

Convenience

Our clients see it as advantageous to trade money for the service we provide. Rather than spending the time and effort necessary to complete these tasks, they would rather pay someone else to do them. Perhaps, they are paid several hundred dollars per hour. It is a profitable convenience for them to pay someone else to do that job while they spend time making their living. Perhaps the client's leisure time is precious to them, and she'd love to pay someone instead of using her time to complete the task. I'm grateful she wants to have someone else do it. We service providers don't argue— this is why we have a service business!

It is important to determine from the very beginning *what type of client would be your best client?* I know many of would just say, "Well, I want to have the type of client that pays me when I'm finished!" Certainly, we'd all like that to be a characteristic of our target client, but what else is special about them?

In business marketing circles, this dream client is called your "avatar." It is an invented person that has all the characteristics you'd like in your best client. For instance, are you hoping to offer your services to pregnant women who can't clean their houses until after the baby comes? Or to the busy, self-employed man who spends most of his days in a Starbucks, emailing clients across the country, and can't take time to clean his own car?

Think about your service. Who would most likely secure your services? Why would she want someone else to do what she might be able to do herself? What is she hoping to get out of the deal with you? What "pain point" will your service alleviate for your client? (Remember, we talked about pain points earlier (p. 93)?

This thinking exercise will help you when you begin thinking about how to "sell" your business to prospective clients. You'll need to know their motivation for seeking the service, so that you can share that exact benefit to them (see *What to Promote*, p. 93).

Your clients are the entire reason you can have a business like you do. They are your lifeblood, so you must treat them as such.

Always use "sir" or "ma'am" until told not to. Some clients feel uncomfortable with these terms, but once you've used it, they've gotten the message that you have a high respect for them. I'm from the South so this comes naturally for me.

Be professional with them at all times. No matter what kind of day you've had or what personal problems you may be experiencing, don't bring them up to your client. They don't need to be worried about your personal problems; you want them to only focus on the quality of your work.

Trust your clients, and they will trust you. My business never accepts payment for our service until after the work is completed and the client is satisfied. This practice makes my newer employees a bit nervous until they've seen it work over time. Our policy does two things: it helps the client setting up the appointment to have a high degree of trust in my business right from the start, and it is an external motivator for me and my employees to stay true to the agreement for which we've been contracted.

NOTE: "But what if my client doesn't pay me?" Our no-payment-until-after policy raises eyebrows sometimes, but it's turned out very well for me. Yes, of the 1000+ vehicles we detail every year, probably two skip out without payment. However, I've decided not to reverse this policy and lose the benefits it affords my business, for the sake of a few flakey clients. In our business, we have activated a few guidelines to minimize the times we could be "taken."

Renew Mobile Detailing's Common Sense Safe Guards:

- **If you're not meeting at a person's home or office, require payment beforehand.** Once, our detailer met a man to detail his truck in an abandoned parking lot. After the client inspected the work, he stuffed some cash in my detailer's hands and quickly sped away in his nice, shiny truck. When he counted the money, he was short $100!

- **If the phone call setting the appointment sounded "shady."** Sometimes, we get a "hint" of something not quite right on the phone, especially if we find the client haggling over the cost. In those instances, we may give another call to the client "confirming" the appointment details and repeating the cost for the service. (If there is any hint of danger, see the *Protection of Employees*, p. 153.)

- **If a third party is paying, and it's unclear at all who's paying, require payment before beginning.** We've had instances where a roommate got sick in his car; the roommate has agreed to pay, but the car owner is setting the appointment. We require the roommate pay up front in these cases.

When a potential new client calls, you want to treat them professionally and not appear too eager to set an appointment. Remember, they want to know that you're well-established and in-demand as a service provider.

Don't say something like, "Thanks for calling, you're the first call all day," or "Yes, our schedule is wide open; you can pick any day you want!" These responses cause the client to think: "Wow, if nobody else is calling them, maybe they're not that good?"

Instead, you want to answer the phone, describe your services, and set an appointment. As you're looking at your empty calendar, you might say something like, "Let's see, I have an opening Tuesday morning around 8:30 or Wednesday afternoon beginning at 1:30. Would either of those time slots be convenient for you?"

This line of speaking promotes the idea of scarcity. You are saying to the client, "You are very important to me, but my other clients are important too. Here's where I can fit you in." Your client is thinking, "Wow, I'm glad I called when I did. If I'd waited until tomorrow, these slots may have been taken."

If she says, "I'm sorry, could we begin at 230PM on Wednesday instead." Answer, "Yes, ma'am. I'll make that work for you." This shows your effort to please the client and make some extra effort to "make it work" for her.

Your clients should know that you will perform your service to them in a timely and efficient manner. The finished product should be a mirror image of what was promised, and even go beyond their expectations.

Arrive on time, or even early to your appointment. I tell my employees to always have a book to read or something else to do if they arrive before the client does. It gives the client confidence in your business when you're running ahead-of-schedule.

Under-promise, but over-deliver. Once you have done exactly what has been contracted by the client and you know their final inspection will pass with flying colors, do one more thing. You don't want your client to be merely satisfied, but over-whelmed with the quality of your work. I want my clients to be "wow-ed" when they come back to their vehicle!

Guarantee your work. Have as your goal the complete satisfaction of your client with your work. Don't put away your equipment before they have given final approval. You don't want them to feel uncomfortable making you get everything out again to fix one missed area. Occasionally, you'll have unreasonable clients, but it's a rarity. (If it happens, see the *Difficult Clients* section below, p. 113.)

Not all clients are created equal! Some are very understanding and kind; others are...special.

The "I-Could-Do-That" Client. Some clients have a specific way they like their property handled. Many times, they say something like, "Well, I could do this myself, but..." they don't have time, energy, patience. Most service businesses like yours and mine *could be* done by our clients, but for whatever reason, they've hired us to do it. I teach my employees to just smile and nod and continue to do things the way I've trained them to do. I tell them to certainly pay extra attention to those areas pointed out by the client (the "pain points," p. 93), but don't get so far off task that you can't finish the whole job.

The Talkative Client. Some clients will enjoy talking to you, their captive audience, for hours on end. Endure it for a while, but you'll have to excuse yourself to complete the work, because you have other clients who need your attention as well. Try saying, "Well, that's interesting but I've got to get a move on, after all, (said with a smile) this is what you're paying me for!"

The All-Up-in-Your-Business Client. You'll find clients who want to know the entire process of your operation. "Interesting! Why do you do it that way?" After some time, you'll need to use the above escape phrase too, so you can get back to work.

The "No Go" Client. Every once in a while, we'll get a client who cannot be pleased in any way. Perhaps we've gone over the same area several times and he just cannot be pleased. We must weigh the value of this client against the cost of time and effort to please him. If it seems no matter what we do, we'll never please him, he is a "no go" client; there's no going forward with him. We need to let him go, even if it means not being paid for the job.

 **The Client You Have to Fire.** Some clients, like the one above, are more trouble than the benefits they offer to your business. They require more time, effort, and anguish than they are worth in cash. There is also something to be said for firing clients so that your good employees like to work for you! However, this is something that really should only be dealt with by you as the business owner, not your employees.

Try something like this. Muster up as much respect as you can, and speak in a clear voice. *"I'm sorry, sir, but I'm afraid the service our company provides will not be able to meet your expectations. Our goal is to have satisfied clients, and I can see you are clearly not satisfied. What would you see as a fair price to pay for what we've already done?"* Take what you can get, and move on to the next client.

A Real Example: One of my detailers worked on a client's car for four hours one day (normally this service is completed in three hours). The client was still not pleased but my detailer had to leave the client's office to not miss his next appointment. My employee told me the situation, so I called the client to ask if I could come out personally the following day to address the "missed" areas. He agreed, so the next day I spent an additional two hours on the car. He came out and immediately found a speck on the door panel and exclaimed, "Unacceptable!"

I said (and you can use these same words): "Sir, I'm going to have to leave now. *I'm afraid the service our company provides will not be able to meet your expectations. Our goal is to have satisfied clients, and I can see you are clearly not satisfied.* We've spent a total of five hours on your vehicle now; I certainly will not be charging you the full price. *What would you see as a fair price to pay for what we've already done?*" He ended up paying about 2/3 of the original price, but I would have taken zero just to be rid of this no-go client!

Please note: I was courteous and professional. No one who heard an accurate account of the conversation could say I was unreasonable. This way, if Mr. No Go got online and gave a terrible review, I had some facts to show my side of the story.

MONTHLY CLIENTS

Depending on the service area of your business, you may want to offer a monthly service to your clients. You'll have to see what fits your business best.

Set up an auto-payment with their credit or debit card. This gives you more of a guarantee that these monthly payments are going into your checking account automatically. It's a nice feeling!

The "set it and forget it" aspect is appealing to your client. Once it's set up, they don't have to worry about calling and setting up an appointment; it's one less thing they have to worry about. You've relieved a "pain point!"

Your monthly clients usually get a discount. Take up to 15% off and the client will be more open to this type of automatic draft arrangement.

Our Monthly Clients: Our detailing business offers a service where our clients pay a monthly fee, automatically drawn from their credit card account. We do a full detail with waxing, shampooing and everything else the first time, then come back to touch up their vehicle every two weeks. We don't wax and shampoo every time, but do everything else we did the first time. This way, our client gets an amazing-looking car every two weeks! It's not terribly difficult for us because it was in amazing shape just two weeks ago. After three months of this cycle, we begin again with a full detail—waxing and shampooing again. Everyone wins!

INVOICING CLIENTS

You'll need to have some way to officially send an invoice to clients for them to pay, or a receipt for them to show they've already paid. All businesses offer this, so to be professional, yours will need to offer it as well. There are several ways to do this.

You can give the client a hand-written receipt when you're there on site. If your client is paying you on site, you can have an invoice pad (you can get one at any office supply store or even Wal-mart) that you fill out by hand. Usually, it has a carbon copy for your records too.

You can send them an invoice or receipt via email. You can find professional-looking invoice & receipt templates online, or even in Microsoft Word. Just fill in your company's info, save it as a copy, and rework it for each client. I like this method because you are sure to get their email address for future marketing reminders.

Your financial software (like QuickBooks) has this automatically built in. In this case, you just fill in the client's individual information and the description of the services performed. Then, you send the invoice directly from the software to the client's email address.

COMPLAINTS

"You can't please everyone!" But, honestly, none of us are perfect. Whether it's the fault of the client or the fault of your business (you or your employees), complaints are bound to happen. How will you handle them?

Listen to the client without interruption, except for clarification. As a professional business owner, you are concerned that each of your clients receives the quality of service you promote. You want to know if there are any aspects of your service that are below your standards. As you listen to your client's complaint, keeping this in mind will go far to help you respond in a kind, professional manner. As a side benefit, you get to understand the attitude of the client more clearly as you listen.

Pay attention first for the client's feelings—angry, apologetic ("I hate to complain but..."), disappointed. Then ask questions to understand the specifics of the  complaint. Some clients will say, "The service just wasn't what I expected," but with this comment, I don't know what's been missed or how to fix the problem. Ask for specific areas they saw which were not up to par. "The windows still have some gunk in the corners." A complaint like this is specific enough to address.

Let the client know if the complaint is within or outside the scope of your service. Some complaints are based on what the client expected from the service, but were not necessarily included in the service. For example, our detailing company does not include cleaning of the engine nor undercarriage of the vehicle. Most of our clients don't mind that these areas are not addressed, but some do. We try to let them know in the beginning what is covered and what is not, but we're not always successful.

If their expectation is outside the scope of your service, apologetically explain, but don't put them in a bad light. Don't say, "I'm sorry you didn't understand;" say

"I'm sorry that wasn't explained thoroughly. We didn't know that was an expectation."

If, however, their expectation *was* to be included but *was missed...*

Determine the best option for satisfying the client. You can (1) return to the client and take care of what was missed, (2) discount the cost of this present service, or (3) give a discount the next time they order a service from you. Let the client know their satisfaction is your highest concern, and ask them to let you know which option is most agreeable for them. In my experience, when I've presented these options, I've never had a bad review from a client, and many of them have become repeat clients!

PAYMENT FOR SERVICES RENDERED

You're probably not **B**uilding **Y**our **O**wn **B**usiness just to have something to do; you want to get paid! So, how are you going to handle it?

Decide if you'll be paid before the service, after the service, or require a deposit before the service. I have already covered some of my reasons for our business policy about being paid after the service is complete (see p. 109), but you'll have to decide if this is right for your business. It is perfectly acceptable to require a deposit for the service, especially if you must buy materials ahead of time to complete the work. As you are deciding how to handle this question, I encourage you to base your decision on your best clients, not the worst. Don't be afraid of not being paid; assume they're good people.

Will you accept cash, check, card, or a combination? Give your clients as many options as they can to pay you. I've covered earlier how to set up your business to accept credit cards (see p. 48). Cash can be deposited into your bank account and immediately available, checks usually take a day or so, and credit cards take 2-3 business days. You will also have to pay a fee to accept most credit cards.

What if a client said he was going to pay via credit card, but has not? You must take this on a case by case basis. For individuals, I will usually call them the day after the service and say something like, *"I just wanted to call to make sure you were pleased with the service and to take care of payment if you're ready."* Don't ever accuse the client, but always build in an acceptable way out in your comments. *"I know we're all really busy but I haven't seen your payment come through, so I was calling to see if you had received your emailed invoice yet?"* If you can't get him on the phone, just leave a message with some of the wording I've used in these examples.

You can also send an emailed invoice again, if you haven't already. I also have a standard text message I send to clients who haven't paid yet with a link to the credit card provider to pay from their phone.

Here is an example text to use:

Hello Ms. Jones,

Feel free to give me a call with your credit card info or just use the following link to pay for your detailing services yesterday. The total is $235. Tips are not required but appreciated. Just leave the invoice number blank.

http://bit.blahblahbl/ah

Steve Young w/ Renew Mobile Detailing

Give your clients the benefit of the doubt. Most of my clients have just forgotten, or some have even gone out of town. In your communication with the client, always assume they're going to pay you. Don't accuse them of wrongdoing. We detail over 1000 cars a year, but we only get stiffed maybe two times a year. See our *Common Sense Safeguards* on page 110 for more info.

SETTING AND MEETING CLIENT EXPECTATIONS

You will find that most conflicts, whether they are in a marriage, business, or relationship, are caused by *unclear or unmet expectations*. That's why knowing (and helping to set) the client's expectations is vital.

Be as clear as possible during initial conversations about what your service covers

and *what it does not.* It can be a bit difficult to do this if you are talking to potential clients many times a day and are quickly running through your sales pitch. When the conversation is close to the end, and you've made the initial appointment, quickly recapping the details of what you will provide can never be a bad idea. If you send a written proposal, all the better! (See *Example Proposal*, p. 192.)

Touch on the expectations again *the day of* the service appointment before you begin. You have one more chance to set the expectations before performing the service. Before they begin working on

the vehicle, I have my detailers ask their client, "Are there any areas you see that need special attention?" This simple question helps with clarifying her expectations.

After the service is completed, ask the client to inspect the work to make sure you are spot on with her expectations. Make the client as comfortable as possible during this phase of the interaction. You want her to know your main objective is her satisfaction, and you'll stay as long as necessary to make sure she's pleased. I tell my detailers to *not* put away their equipment before this final inspection, so the client knows we're ready to address all her concerns immediately.

SUPPLIES & EQUIPMENT
Tools of the Trade

My father used to say, "You need the right tool for the right job!" Having the right tools can make your job much easier and help you be more efficient with your time. Getting these tools and keeping them in working order will assure you don't have the expense of buying them again sooner than you need to.

MAINTAINING YOUR EQUIPMENT

When you buy new equipment, be sure to register them with the manufacturer so your warranty is in effect. Keep the manuals and receipts in a file for quick retrieval when necessary. Review the maintenance recommendations and mark your calendar for maintenance dates.

Keeping equipment in good working order will allow you to work with clients without interruption on the job. There is nothing like the frustration of having a critical piece of equipment fail on the job, and having to make excuses to the client about why the job was not completed on time! Instances like this make you scream in your head: "If only I had changed the oil in my generator last week!"

Be sure to store and transport your equipment with its care in mind. Don't throw tools or other equipment in your trunk, but treat them with care. Equipment that is well cared for requires fewer repairs. This practice will save time, money, and headaches!

REPAIRING YOUR EQUIPMENT, OR REPLACING IT

Accidents do happen, so when tools need repair, you want to be ready. What do you do when something breaks, or stops working? Your goal as you look for a solution is to find out if it's something simple you can repair yourself, or if a professional is required, or if it's

not worth repairing and should be replaced.

Many times, the manual will have a troubleshooting guide in the back. Look through the symptoms to see what recommendations you can follow.

Check on the internet by describing the problem. I have found YouTube videos that address my exact issue. Sometimes, I've learned how to fix the problem myself!

Depending on the importance of the equipment to completing your job, the timing may be more important than the cost of the repair. For instance, if you can't work at all without a piece of equipment, you may want to buy a replacement before the other one gets repaired. That way, you still have a way to make the money needed to pay for the repair!

Check with your state or county for any reports you must file regarding your equipment. In Tennessee, we have an annual report called "Tax Schedule 'B'" that must be filed. It lists all the equipment I own, complete with serial numbers and current value. It is used to determine the worth of my business, so they can tax me accordingly.

If you don't fill it out, they will "estimate" how much your business is worth, and it seems their estimate is usually much higher than reality. So, it would be in your best interest to fill out the report every year!

Where Is It?

If you have employees and you supply your employees with equipment and tools to use, you need a system to keep up with who has what. When they first get their equipment, I have my employees sign an equipment list to show what they've taken, so that when their employment ends, I'll have a record of what I need to receive back from them.

You may want to have such details as which pieces of equipment are with which employees (even down to the serial number). This way, there will be no discussion about whose equipment is whose. It will also help when filling out the government report mentioned above!

COMPETITION
Who Else is Out There?

You're probably not the only business in your area doing the type of work your business does. You do have competitors. What should you do about them?

Learn *from* them. Know that if they are out in the marketplace, they've done some of the same things you've had to do. If they've been there longer, they've done some things you haven't learned to do yet. See how much you can do to learn about their business. Visit their website to see what it looks like. Learn what services they offer, what prices they charge, and what geographical areas they cover.

This is actually something you will do in the first phase, before you choose a service area to do business in (see p. 15). You want a "blue ocean" market, not a "red ocean" market. A red ocean already has a lot of competitors fighting each other for the same clients. The blood from the fight has turned the ocean red! A blue ocean market has plenty of clients for everyone. (See also the Winning Attitude *Abundance Mentality*, p. 66.)

Learn *about* them. Look up their business on some of the review sites like Yelp or Google Business. See what people are saying about them. Do they do a good job? Are their employees timely and professional? Are they trustworthy? Would you like to do business with them if you were seeking their service?

Seek to **B**uild **Y**our **O**wn **B**usiness by making your competitor's weaknesses your strengths! (See also, p. 15.)

Build your business by learning about their weaknesses. Think about this for a moment: If you

were going to give your competitors some advice about what they could do to improve their business based on the complaints in the reviews, what would you say? Write these things down on a list. Now, look at the list. *You've just written a list of key areas your business can focus on to make your business better than your competitor's.* Be sure all your marketing states that these qualities are the hallmark of your business.

Cooperate and share overflow customers with your trusted competitors. As you grow, you may get so many clients that you can't service them sufficiently, or in a timely manner. This can happen especially when you have a full schedule and a new client calls with an emergency. Rather than tell them there's nothing I can do to help them, I'll recommend my competitor. I always say, "Tell him Steve sent you," so he'll know where the referral came from. I've had many of these callers thank me profusely and promise to call me for their future needs. I now have two other competitors who refer to me on a regular basis when they're full!

EMPLOYEES I
Hiring & Training

This is a Bonus Chapter because not every new business is ready for employees. But if you are, you'll find some valuable information in this chapter to help you get employees and train them to do what you want them to do. The following chapter will go into the management of your employees (see *Employees II*, p. 148).

WHY HIRE EMPLOYEES

Employees provide a way to multiply your efforts. Instead of working with only one client at a time, an additional employee allows you to work with two clients at the same time. Each pays you for the work, but after paying the employee, you as the owner still come away with more profit for the day.

Employees allow you, as the owner, to do what only you can do. They provide you the time, focus, and energy to do what needs to happen in your business that an employee can't do. For example, while you're detailing a car, you must answer the phone to deal with future, past, or potential clients. Having an employee allows you to focus on the tasks of working "on" your business, not just working "in" your business. (See *Where are You Working?*, p. 175.)

Employees provide security for unforeseen circumstances. Perhaps you get sick and can't do physical work for a week. An employee can continue serving clients while you are home answering the phone and making appointments.

WHEN TO HIRE EMPLOYEES

Only hire employees when you must hire employees. As your client base grows, you must hire enough employees to meet the demands of your clients. There is a constant tension between scheduled appointments, wait time, and the number of employees.

You don't want:
1. Clients to wait an inordinate amount of time before their service is completed.
2. Clients to move on to another service provider and you lose their business.
3. Employees to not have enough to do and look for a job somewhere else.

My hiring rule of thumb is to begin looking for a new employee when these two conditions are true:
- I've lost three or more clients in the same week because I didn't have enough room in the schedule to meet their needs, <u>and</u>
- The next month has historically seen an uptick in scheduled clients (i.e. we're coming into the "high" season).

The "high" season for us is March through October, with the low season being the winter months. If I begin seeing three or more clients per week moving on to other service providers and it's October, I will *not* hire another employee. November will likely see a downward trend in client appointments. I don't want to hire someone I can't keep busy the first week he comes to work.

 It takes several weeks from beginning to end of the employee acquisition process to have an employee "boots on the ground," fully ready to service clients. I must anticipate what the client load will be like when he has finished his training and is ready to work, so he will have a full load of work his first week.

HOW TO HIRE EMPLOYEES

You must find the employees.

I was surprised that finding employees was much harder than I had imagined. I've found there are many people looking for jobs, who (apparently) don't really want to work! For that reason, we've developed a **5-Step Process** to find employees.

Step 1. *Advertise* – You must let others know you're hiring if you want to get a new employee. Talk with friends about needing to hire someone, post an ad in Craigslist and your Facebook page, and/or local bulletin boards at the public library or other places your potential hires may frequent. Talk also to your current employees about people they might recommend.

Here is an example of one of our Craigslist ads:

Car Detailer (Nashville)

Renew Mobile Detailing seeking car detailer for mobile detailing & fleet wash service. See website at www.renewdetailing.com.

Candidate must:
- be honest & dependable, and have good social skills for interaction with clients.
- have own reliable transportation and personal cell phone.
- be willing to work hard with a good attitude.
- have a clean record (including driving record) - background check required.
-must be able to lift, bend, be on your feet for long periods of time, and tolerate hot and cold weather.

Good pay. Experience a plus, but will train right candidate. Reply with resume or job history. Include phone number, address, references.

Step 2. *Ask for a Resume or Work History* – You would be surprised at the number of responses we get from a Craigslist ad with something like: "Hey, here's my number 555-555-5555. Give me a call."

Step 3. *Examine the resume and work history.* Are there any misspellings? Have they jumped from job to job? Have they had any service jobs before? These are not deal-breakers, but items you'll want to notice as you look through this document. If you're pleased with what you find, then next...

Step 4. *Conduct the phone interview* – Call the potential employee, give your name and company name, explain you've received their resume or work history and wanted to talk with them further about the job, and ask if this a good time. If it's not a good time, set another time for the phone interview. Ask any clarifying questions from your reading of the resume or work history. Give an overview of the job—what the company does, what the job entails, hours and days per week expected, wages offered, etc. Ask if she has any questions about the job for you. If this goes well, move on to step 5, *interview the potential employee.*

RED FLAG WARNING – If the phone number on the resume is not their own number, but the number of his girlfriend, mother, or roommate, be very careful hiring this person. If you can't connect with them directly, they will not be a good employee.

You must interview the employees.

This is Step 5 of the interviewing process—a face-to-face interview with the potential employee. You will learn much about the candidate from this interview.

- *First impressions* – Whatever you feel, just know that this is the impression the future client will feel about this employee's character.
- *Ability to speak and interact with clients* – How comfortable does he seem as he speaks with you?
- *Respect for you as an employer* – If he shows no respect in the interview process, he will *not* be respectful as an employee
- *Is he F.A.T.* – *Faithful, Available, and Teachable?* Will he do the tasks as assigned? Will he be available to fulfill the demands of

your work schedule? Will he be correctable in the training process, and even later receiving correction as an employee?

We always set the interview location at a nearby restaurant instead of at our house. If the interview does not go well, we don't want the interviewee to know where we live. If the interview is canceled we have not spent a long time driving.

Texting Beforehand

We have been surprised how many potential employees get to this stage and do not show up to the face to face interview. To have one more step of confirmation for a potential employee, and to save us our time and effort waiting for an interview that will never happen, we've designed this additional step.

The potential employee must text my phone an hour before the interview with a message indicating he still plans to attend the interview. If we don't receive a text, we don't go to the interview.

During the interview:

1. *Go over in depth what is expected of the employee.* I have a document with all this information listed. I give a copy to the potential employee and I keep a copy. We walk through it line by line. It includes days and hours per week he'll be required to work; days off for sickness or other issues; pay rate and pay schedule; client interaction; expected communication with you or the supervisor (phone, text, email, etc.); uniforms or other dress requirements.

2. *Ask for any questions from the potential employee.* If he's been asking questions throughout the interview, his concerns may have already been addressed, but ask the question anyway. It's important to make sure he feels comfortable with you, and for you to feel comfortable with him.

> **GOLDEN TIP:** In my experience, most disagreements (in the workplace, in relationships, in churches, or wherever) occur because of unclear or unmet expectations. For this reason, spending time clearly outlining expectations of the employee and his expectations of you as the employer will avoid many pitfalls in the future employer/employee relationship! (See also, p. 121.)

IMPORTANT: At this point, you must decide if the candidate is a potential employee or not. If there is any hesitation, or she has said something in the interview that made you think she won't fit in your business, let her go. Pick up your things, and say something like, "Okay, that's all I have for you right now. I'll give you a call tomorrow about the job."

As a faithful employer, do the upright thing and call her the next day. Tell her that after doing several interviews (if you've honestly done other interviews), you've decided to go with another candidate. You wish her well in her job search, and hang up. Treating even potential employees with respect will only come back to help your business.

If, however, you *do* like the candidate, then proceed to the next step in the interview process, and...

3. *Go over the necessary paperwork.* You'll need
    - a **W-4 form** complete with address and social security number for payroll (free, downloadable form from www.irs.gov),
    - an **I-9 form** to show she is a US citizen or has legal papers to work in this country (free, downloadable form from www.irs.gov),
    - a **permission form for background check** (it's important to be able to let your clients know you do background checks on each employee),

NOTE: When you pass the background check permission form to the candidate, say something like, "Will we find any surprises here?" This gives the candidate a chance to "come clean" and tell you up front if there are any illegal activities that may come up during the background check. If they indicate no surprises will come up, you still need to complete the background check fully.

Being able to tell your clients that all your employees submit to a background check will only build client confidence. Plus, if the candidate is lying, you need to find this out as soon as possible.

In my business, lying is an immediately dismissible offense. See my story of an employee I caught in a lie later (p. 171).

You can find several companies online for your background check needs. If you have a payroll company, they may be able to provide this service. The cost can be as little as $25 per employee. They will provide the permission form for you to give to the candidate.

- a **direct deposit form** with his banking information for payroll purposes if you want to offer this service (For me, it's less of a hassle if the paycheck goes directly to his bank account, and I don't have to worry about physical checks.)

- My business also adds a **non-compete contract** for her to sign before beginning the training process. This document states that she can't leave your business and start her own competing business using the skills you taught her.

Non-Compete Contract. This is an optional form for your business, but you may consider using it. You can find several free non-compete forms on the internet, but one prepared by an attorney may be more enforceable. Our non-compete states that for a period of 2 years or a distance of 50 miles, the former employee cannot start his own detailing business. Since we're a local business, any business started that far away is not a direct competitor.

- Another optional form our business uses is a **supplies and equipment list.** Our new employee signs this form when he's given his own supplies and equipment. It outlines everything he's been given and states he is responsible for its return at the end of his employment.

Remember, **if you are unsure** and need to think further before offering her the job, tell her you'll get in touch when you've made a decision and leave the meeting. **If you're sure you do not want to hire her**, do the same thing but tell her you'll call the following day with your decision. It's not fair to make her wait for this "possible" job.

HOW TO TRAIN EMPLOYEES

In any training, there are three phases of the training.

Explanation & Demonstration – I tell you & show you how to do it.
Imitation & Clarification – You do it like I did it, and I watch you.
Initiation & Correction – You do it, and I correct and answer questions.

You will need to develop these three phases around the specific service tasks of your business. I have outlined below exactly how we do it at Renew Mobile Detailing. As you read, note the three phases and how we address them over and over. Repetition is the key to learning.

Our Training Process. In our detailing business, the first day of training begins in my garage at 8am. I go through each of the chemicals we use, explaining their various uses, and concentrations (we dilute some with water). I know they're not going to remember all this after one explanation, but you have to begin somewhere! Then, I take them through each of the tools and machines we use—the vacuum, the carpet extractor, the generator, various brushes, etc. I explain how to use and service each one if needed.

Afterward, they detail a few cars with my head detailer. He is very patient with them while walking through the first two phases of training. He explains what he's doing in one area of the car while showing them at the same time, then he asks them to do the same area on the other side of the vehicle. He checks their work as he also gives them hints about being more efficient and speedy in their efforts.

At the end of the day, I talk with the detailer who trained the new employee and ask how it went. I pay attention to the skills learned, but I'm even more interested in the attitude of the new employee; I ask, "Is he teachable?" I can train anyone to detail a car, but if they're not open to correction, I can't teach them anything!

My job is to run a business, not make someone job worthy. I want employees who already have the quality of "teachableness." (I'm not really sure if it's a word, but it works for me!)

Then I call the new employee and ask how he thought he did during the day. Again, I listen for teachability and attitude. I give constructive feedback, and clarify my expectations of the employee if they are not clear.

The next day, he goes for the day with a different detailer. With this new trainer, he'll learn new techniques and strategies for cleaning a car; a whole different set of hints. If he did really well the day before, I'll ask this trainer to talk with him about client interaction. If appropriate, the new employee will take the lead in greeting & introduction to the client, asking for the client's expectations or areas which need extra focus, and the final inspection after completion of the detail.

Again, at the end of the day, I'll speak with the trainer about any areas of concern. I want to know how the trainee did with the client. At this point, I'll ask the trainer if he feels the new employee is ready to go on his own. It's rare, but I've had some new employees ready after just two days of training. I'll speak with the new employee about any additional concerns or questions he has. I'll ask if he feels he's ready to go to a client on his own.

More times than not, I'll have him spend another day with the first trainer again. The trainer will take a background position as far as client interaction is concerned. He will watch the trainee handle all direct contact with the client.

With the new employee knowing that the following day will be his first all-on-his-own day, he'll pay more attention to what he needs to learn during this last day of training.

The next day, he goes on his first solo assignment. I only schedule one detailing client for the day so he doesn't feel rushed to get off to his second appointment. I instruct him to call with any question whatsoever. He can call me for anything business related, or one of the training detailers about anything related to cleaning the vehicle. This needs to be a "no-judgement" time for asking questions. All my training detailers know this; don't make him feel bad for asking questions.

After they have received their training, the new employee may need her own set of tools, equipment, and other supplies. At that time, I ask them to sign the list of all these materials they are receiving. Then I have a signed document showing the items they've received, and at the same time, a list of items they will need to return at the end of their employment (p. 142).

YOUR COMPANY "CULTURE"

Our family lived in the country of Mexico for over a decade. My children grew up with two cultures—the American culture within the four walls of our house, and the Mexican culture everywhere else! We loved the Mexican culture, but we knew there were differences when compared to the American culture. For example, attention to punctuality was not a value in Mexican culture, where it was very important in the American culture.

Every business has its own "culture" as well, most easily explained as the "expectations" of the business for those within it. Each employee spends time in the beginning learning what these expectations are and how strong each expectation is. Most people within a culture don't even realize their expectations exist, until the moment when their expectations are not met.

A good business owner will have clearly written expectations of his employees—his business culture clearly defined. He will include these expectations in the orientation of his new hires. (See *Training Employees*, p. 142.)

Business culture really exists and is being constantly discovered. The wise business owner will note these discoveries and update his employees often.

[I thank my friend Derek Evans, co-owner of *Project 615* (www.project615.org), an awesome t-shirt design shop here in Nashville, for suggesting that I deal with the Business Culture in this book.]

EMPLOYEES II
Managing & Firing

Once you get the "perfect" employee, she still needs to be managed. You have to help her do what she was hired to do. This chapter will give you several helpful hints to manage her well!

RESPECT

The quality of respect is a key factor in relating with your employees. They must demonstrate respect toward you, but you also need to show respect toward them. Besides the legal ramifications, it's just the right thing to do. Each should respect the other.

Respect time. If you set a time to meet your employee and you're going to be late, the courteous thing to do is to call and let him know. You expect this of him as well.

Respect ears. There is no place for raising your voice toward your employee, and he certainly should not raise his voice toward you. Disagreements and correction should be handled without escalated emotion. The goal of correction is better performance, and raising your voice rarely results in better performance. (See *Correction*, p. 164.)

Respect clients. Always speak respectfully about your clients. If you speak disrespectfully about a client with your employee, this attitude can spill over to the employee's performance with the client. The goal with the client is to maintain a good relationship. Remarks like these can tear that relationship down.

Respect the business. The employee should exhibit a healthy gratitude for the opportunity to work in your business. You reward good effort with good pay, and the employee should be thankful to be able to work for such a business.

FAIRNESS

Being "fair" has become a word of accusation in the past years. Lawsuits abound over an employee not being treated fairly. You must take care to always treat each employee fairly.

Financially. Be sure to record and pass on all tips an employee has earned. If a mistake has been made on the work log (p. 163), apologize and make the correction as soon as possible. You expect the employee to complete her assignments; she expects you to pay her for the work.

Assignments. When giving out the work assignments, employees on the same level should receive the same treatment. In my business, each new hire begins on the "bottom of the food chain." I try to fill the schedules of the earlier hires before filling the schedules of the later hires. This is explained to the new employees at the beginning. The longer they stay with my business, the more assignment preference is given.

The Difference Between "Unfair" and "Unequal"

Sometimes, employees will cry "unfair" when actually the correct term is "unequal." To treat an employee differently because of his race, gender, religion, or sexual preference is "unfair" and against the law. "Unequal" practices, however, are not the same.

You must realize that not all employees have the same abilities or situations. You must make assignments for each employee to provide the best service to the client whether those assignments appear "fair" or not.

Several factors may contribute to the *appearance* of unfair practices. A slower employee may not get the harder jobs until his speed improves. A newer employee who has not developed his skills as much will not get assignments which need those finer skills. In my business, each employee is told during the interview that those employees who have been with the business the longest will have their schedules filled before those with lesser time with the business.

These are all *unequal* practices, but not *unfair* ones.

COMMUNICATION PROTOCOL

In your business, you will establish rules for your employees to communicate with you in various forms. Here are some suggestions about the type of communication for each form.

Texting – Use texting (or email) for short, specific information you need your employee to know, especially anything involving numbers: addresses, phone numbers, prices. NEVER use sarcasm in a text message. The goal is clarity of communication. If the employee must interpret what is meant by your text, she may arrive at a different meaning. Also, never attempt to administer correction or discipline of an employee using a text (see *Face to Face*, p. 152).

Texting Protocol in My Business

We use texting daily in my business for

- *I text assignments the night before.* Some time between 7 and 8pm, the employee will receive the specifics of his assignments for the following day. This includes time of appointment, address, type of job & cost, client name & phone, and any special instructions. The employee must respond with something simple like "Got it" to let me know he has received the assignment.
- *The employee texts his arrival and departure times for the assignment.* The employee will text me when he arrives on site, and again when he departs so I can know where each employee is all throughout the day. The departure text also contains if the client was pleased with the job and how he plans to pay—card, check, or cash, as well as if there was a tip included in the check.

Phone Calls – For long or involved instruction, use phone calls instead of texts. The back and forth texting can allow more opportunities for misinterpretation, while the back and forth dialogue on the phone brings clarity.

Emails – Use email for general instruction or announcements to all employees, and to send specific documents to them. In my business, I send the recorded work logs (p. 163) each pay period showing a detailed list of their assignments and how that resulted in their check amount.

Face to Face – There is no substitute for the clarity of a face to face conversation. This type of communication is the only one which really builds trust between employer and employee. *Always* use this form of communication for any negative or corrective communication. (See *Correction*, p. 164, and *Firing*, p. 166.)

CLIENT/EMPLOYEE INTERACTION

Your business may or may not require that your employees interact with clients, but if it does, here are some tips for making that interaction the most positive it can be. I am never more pleased when I read a review of my business than when the well-pleased client begins by praising my employee!

Be Professional – First impressions are hard to re-make. Employees should be dressed in uniform (if applicable) and otherwise have an appearance which inspires trust. You know your clients, so you'll know what appearance "sets them off." The employee should not use the client's first name, but "Mr._____" or "Ms. _____."

Be Nice – Teach your employees to treat your clients like the real people they are. The client herself may be late for the appointment, may have misunderstood what was included, or may have had a bad day already. The employee's calm approach to ease her mind will go far toward a pleasant interaction (and a better tip!).

Be Clear – The employee should patiently explain what can and cannot be completed (if that's in question). He should instill confidence in the client that his desire is to do a quality job. (If a client is angry, the employee should call you. See *Protection of Employees*, p. 153.)

PROTECTION OF EMPLOYEES

Just as you cannot have a business without clients, you cannot grow your business without employees. Your employee must know that "you have her back." She must trust you to do the equitable thing when there are problems with a client.

If the Client is Angry – If the employee becomes uncomfortable with the questions from the client, he should offer to call you, his employer, for intervention. You must take (or make) the call and settle any differences in expectations with the client. The employee then feels valued and protected by you.

If a Client is Accusing the Employee of Theft – In this event, listen carefully to the client's concerns, offering to speak directly to the employee about any missing items. At the same time, display complete trust in your employee, stating all employees have passed a background check (See *Background Check*, p. 140). Don't throw your employee "under the bus." Assure the client you will get back to him in a timely manner after speaking with the employee. Clarify with your employee to see if he remembers the item and then attempt to rectify the situation. It may be worth paying for something damaged or lost, instead of a disenchanted client or risking a bad review.

From My Business – The Lost Keys

A client called (not accusingly) about a missing set of car keys. This was a friend of mine so he had given me the secret location of his house key, and where he would leave the truck keys inside the kitchen. My detailer was to go into the house, get the keys, and after detailing the truck, return the keys to the place where he found them. My friend called me and was pleased with the work but unable to find the keys to another vehicle that were in the kitchen earlier.

I called my employee. He told me everything he had done, but he had not seen these other keys mentioned by my friend. I called my friend and reported everything my detailer had said. I offered to have some new keys made; he said he'd look some more before it came to that.

> He called a day or so later saying he had found his keys in his truck tool box. He had evidently dropped them there by mistake!
>
> From this incident, my client was assured that we have an honorable business (I had offered to pay for replacement keys even though we were not at fault), and that I trusted my employees. My employee's trust in me grew because he felt valued. Wins all around!

If There is Danger – If at any time, the client gets violent or threatening, the employee should know to leave the premises immediately. If the employee feels she is in danger, she should pack up and leave. No client is worth endangering your employee.

PAYING DECISIONS

Before you hire employees, you'll need to decide how your employee's payment will be determined.

Hourly or By the Job – If your employees will be coming to a central location and work for so many hours per week, payment by the hour is a convenient way to go—for example, working in a repair shop. However, if your employee is going to the client and doing the work on site, either paying him hourly or paying by the job may work well.

Training Pay – During the time of training, will the employee get a regular hourly wage, or something else? If you're paying by the job, perhaps a percentage of the regular job payment is in order.

Travel and Other Expenses – If your employee must travel to clients using her own vehicle, you must decide if and how you will reimburse her for these travel expenses. If they must purchase supplies on their own, how will they be reimbursed?

An Example of Payment in My Business

Our employees go to the client's home or worksite to detail their vehicles. My employees are paid based on a percentage of what the client pays. He knows before he even begins the job what he will be making. He knows Renew's standard of cleanliness and over time will get more efficient in achieving this standard. Over time, he begins to realize that as he improves his service speed, essentially, his "by the hour" payment goes up. The better his interaction with the client gets, the more tips he acquires also.

When our employees are in training, they are being trained by other employees on regular client jobs. So, the new employees are really doing on-the-job training. I divide the employee wages percentage portion of the client's cost between the trainer and the trainee 60/40 respectively. Then I give the trainer an extra trainer bonus which brings his total take for the job very near what he would have made had he not been training that day. I don't want the trainer to dread training thinking this "newbee" will be getting 40% of his profit for the job. I give the trainee a training bonus also, but not as much as the trainer. He will receive payment during training, but he will be motivated to do well, so

---

he can go on his first solo job and make 100% of the wages from the job. They also split tips 60/40. For example:

Full Detail Client Cost	*$240 + $20 (tip)*
Wage Percentage (30%)	*$72.00*
Trainer (60% of Wage%)	*$43.20*
	+ $12 (tip)
	+ $20 (training bonus)
	= $75.20
Trainee (40% of Wage%)	*$28.80*
	+ $8 (tip)
	+ $15 (training bonus)
	= $51.80

My employees are not normally reimbursed for travel. The exception is when he must travel outside our normal service radius. In this case, the client pays an extra travel fee which goes directly to the employee. My employees understand that they are being paid well for their work and travel expenses must be planned for by them. Some days, they may have jobs close to their house; other days, far from their house. It all seems to balance out over time.

Each employee also has a generator which needs to be filled with gas once a week or so. They understand that they must pay this cost of roughly $5/week.

PAYMENT SCHEDULE

You will need to determine what your payment schedule will be; once per month, once every two weeks, weekly? Several factors go into making this decision.

Employee Situation – Most employees will find it difficult to go long periods without getting paid. Their personal situation will determine how they handle the gap between paychecks. You would be wise to recognize this reality.

Employer Finances – You need to determine what level of discipline you have as a business owner when it comes to financial habits. As you are paid for services, you must put aside that money designated for paying employees. As payday approaches, if you're not ready for  this amount to come out of your account and deposited to theirs, each payday will be a very stressful day.

From My Business

I have chosen to pay every two weeks. The pay cycle begins on Monday, continues through two weeks to the following Sunday. I then have 5 days to process the payroll with my payroll company (see p. 159 below), so they will receive their checks (or direct deposits) by the following Friday. As diagramed here...

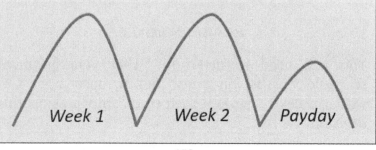

I suggest having a separate bank account called "Payroll." Each time you're paid for a job, put a certain percentage of that income into the Payroll account immediately. This way, when the pay period ends and it's time to pay your employees, the money is already sitting in this account, designated for that purpose.

If you have chosen to have a payroll company do your payroll for you (and I highly recommend this!), usually they will take care of seeing that the state and federal taxes for your employee are paid as well. To me, this alone is worth the monthly payroll fees! The employee portion of these taxes include federal withholding tax, Medicare, and social security. They will also pay the employer's portion of these state and federal taxes.

WORKMAN'S COMP

If you have more than five employees, you'll be required to purchase Workman's Compensation (WC). It comes into play if the employee is hurt while performing his duties for your business. It's fairly expensive, so do your homework before you begin the process. Get bids from several insurance agents to see who can offer the best prices and benefits for your company.

What does Workman's Comp cover?

It covers your employee's medical bills. Similar to medical insurance, Workman's Comp will help with medical bills, usually with some sort of deductible which you cover as the employer. It'd be a good idea to have some amount set aside in a special emergency account for such an occurrence.

It covers your employee's time away from work. As a type of disability  insurance, Workman's Comp pays a weekly wage while the employee is recovering. In extreme cases when the injury results in a permanent disability, it can cover the loss of future income as well.

It covers you, as the employer, from being sued by your employee. Since you have taken responsibility for your employee and his well-being on the job, he gives up his right to sue you if he is hurt on the job. Workman's Comp is a very good coverage for you, the employer.

Like I said before, you're required to have Workman's Comp if you have five employees or more, but even if you have fewer, it may be a good idea to have it. Check with your insurance agent to see what's involved.

PAYMENT ADVANCES

From time to time, an employee may approach you to see about getting an "advance" on his check. Perhaps he has run out of money and needs a small amount to carry him over to the next regularly scheduled check. You will need to determine ahead of time if and how you will grant or deny these requests.

In my business, I will do this for my employee a few times, especially when he first begins working for me. He may not have had a paycheck in a few weeks or months, and needs to have money for gas to even get to his job. I can understand his situation.

If, however, this practice begins becoming a regular occurrence, some strict rules must come into place. Let me offer this as an option for you: Only two extra checks per month for two months, then no advance checks permitted.

Additionally, I only advance the employee what he has already earned. I never advance so much that he is indebted to the business. For one thing, if he ends up quitting or being fired, I don't want to be in the position to try and collect this debt!

TIME OFF

Remember, your employees do have a life outside your business. I encourage you to heartily encourage time off for physical and mental recuperation, and building up the employee's relationships with those he loves. When he comes back, he will be ready to put in some good hours of work, having refocused from his time away.

In my business, we don't have a time off or vacation policy apart from the three considerations below. You may want to develop a more detailed system, but this simple one has worked well for me.

Planned – If the employee has an event in the future which he knows will intersect with his regular working hours, I ask him to let me know at least two weeks ahead of time. I can almost guarantee he will be allowed to take the time off given that amount of notice. Such events include weddings, trips, and family vacations.

Last Minute – Life doesn't always give you two weeks' notice. Perhaps an employee has to take a child to the doctor, or another unforeseen appointment; in this case he should let me know as soon as possible and we must make adjustments. [NOTE: If last minute schedule changes become frequent, and it's affecting employee performance and/or inconveniencing your clients, you'll need to have a strong conversation with your employee. See *Too Much Time Off* below.

Sick Leave – When an employee calls saying he's sick and can't come to work, you must do whatever needs to happen to reschedule his clients. Most clients understand when an employee "calls in sick." Ask enough questions to find out if this "sickness" is self-induced or not. If the employee stayed up late binging on the television, playing video games, or out drinking with friends, these are not "excusable" absences. See *Correction* below (p. 164).

Too Much Time Off – Remember that the reason you have employees is to multiply your services for clients and thus your income. If an employee's requests for time off is causing him to be a part-time employee instead of full-time, you must have a strong conversation with him. You have invested time in training him for a full-time position, devoted a full set of equipment for his use, and have a full-time set of clients for him to service. If he's only servicing half those clients, perhaps a replacement employee is in order.

WORK LOGS

 Keeping a record of your employees' work performance is vital for your business. You can use this log as a record of what work was performed and for what pay. Also, if discrepancies come up after payroll, your employee work log will show the proper documentation regarding where the employee was working on which day and for what pay.

NOTE: In my mobile detailing business, I have a work log for the two-week pay period of each employee. It is broken down by client and shows the date, time, client name, job performed, how many vehicles, vehicle size, cost to client, how they paid, and what the employee made from the job. It also shows tips, travel pay, and any bonuses earned. (See example of work log here).

	A	B	C	D	E	F	
1	Joe	M	T	T	W	F	
2	Date	5/22	5/23	5/23	5/24	5/26	
3	Time (am/pm)	830am		10am	1030am		
4	Client	I Miller	Bridgestone	D Hillis	T Carden	Bridgestone	
5	Size Vehicle (I, II, III)	I	III	I	I	III	
6	Service (BN, BX, F, P)	BN	Z	Z	F	Z	
7	No. of Vehicles	1	1	1	1	1	
8	Cost	$135	$75	$85	$205	$75	
9	Pymt Type	CC	Invoice	Monthly	CC	Invoice	
10	33%	$44.55	$24.75	$28.05	$67.65	$24.75	
11	Tip			$12			
12	Bonus						
13	Travel						
14	Discount	former client					
15	Other Notes						
16	DETAILER	$44.55	$24.75	$40.05	$67.65	$24.75	
17							

CORRECTION OF EMPLOYEES

When I hire employees, I tell them I'm looking for **F.A.T.** employees—**F**aithful, **A**vailable, and **T**eachable! They must be faithful to complete the assignments I give them, available to work the hours of their assignments, and teachable when correction is needed (see p. 137).

DOCUMENTATION: It's in your best interest (and possibly your best legal interest) to document each and every correction and firing event. Just write down the date, place, and incident. Explain what words were stated and decisions reached. For firing, state clearly the reason for the firing.

No one gets everything right every time—we all make mistakes. When an employee makes a mistake, he must be able to receive correction. This word "correction" is not the same as "punishment"—it means retraining, or just reminding. My goal for my employees is correcting the error, not making him feel bad that he made a mistake!

If a client detected the error, I will explain to the employee the phone call I received from the client. I communicate with understanding and I stress that everyone makes mistakes, so that he doesn't feel condemned or defensive. I clarify the correct procedure and make sure he understands what needs to happen in the future. Then, I end the conversation with some positive quality I like about the employee.

When correcting someone (or delivering any type of negative news), it's always a good idea to sandwich your bad news in between two slices of good news. Like this...

If an employee continues to make the same mistakes, or he does not receive correction willingly, some disciplinary action may be in order. Have another face-to-face conversation with the employee (always in person, not by phone, especially not by text or email). Explain again the correction needed; remind him of the previous conversation; explain clearly the action you will take until his performance is up to standard.

Some examples of disciplinary action include less hours to work (resulting in less pay), decrease in paying percentage, ineligibility for bonuses, or some other disciplinary action. Whatever discipline you determine, it must be something that is uncomfortable for the employee. When the "pain" of the discipline becomes greater than the "pain" of correcting his performance, he will change.

NOTE: Each state has disciplinary guidelines or laws for employees. You should check with your **State Labor Office** to find out how you should handle employee discipline and firing.

FIRING EMPLOYEES

It's not a fun process to fire someone, and it should be the last resort. After all, you've spent time and money training this employee, and you'll have to go through this process again to find and retrain her replacement.

I must let you know that most of the time I've had to fire someone, I wished I'd done it earlier. Lesson to learn: when I first start thinking of firing someone, I must take it seriously by either correcting the performance/attitude, or getting on with the firing process.

Reasons for Firing – Why might you need to fire someone? The first reason here is just the last step in the correction process; the other reasons are immediate grounds for firing.

1. *Correction Process Not Successful* – If after going through the correction process outlined above, the employee cannot bring her performance up to standard, you must fire the employee. When clients are not getting what they're paying for, it's not fair to the client. When your other employees see this under-performing employee continue to work for you, their motivation will be undermined. They could wonder, "Why should I work so hard to provide service that is up to standard while this other employee doesn't and still has a job?" For the good of the business, you must fire this under-performing employee.

2. *Dishonest Behavior or Words* – If an employee lies to you or (God forbid) a client, it's immediate grounds for firing. If an employee steals from you or a client, it's immediate grounds for firing. If an employee tries to offer a client a better deal under the table, it's

immediate grounds for firing. (See *Firing Examples* below, p. 171.)

3. *Inappropriate Client Interaction* – If an employee is rude or otherwise disrespectful to the client, you must investigate immediately. If there was an altercation where the client was acting inappropriately, refer to the *Protection of Employees* section above (p. 153). If your employee was indeed acting inappropriately, this may be a fireable offence. Determine if the incident reflects a one-time incident (undue stress from a death in the employee's family, or something like this) or a deep-rooted problem which may occur again.

4. *Unprofitable Performance* – Perhaps your employee is too slow on each job, or cannot handle the work hours and/or work load. Your equipment is being tied up with essentially a part-time employee when a full-time employee is needed. Perhaps you could demote the employee to a part-time or as-needed status. If this is not possible, and you've already used extra training to get them up to speed, you may need to let them go.

Trust

If I can't trust my employee, I can't have him as an employee. If I have caught the employee in a dishonest action, I will always wonder when the next dishonest action will occur. Should I risk the property of my next client with this employee who's already demonstrated dishonesty with another client's property, or my own?

Once trust is lost, the only way it's won back is through consistent trustworthy actions. (This is a life lesson that applies to every relationship!) Am I willing to spend the time and the monitoring effort to allow my employee to win back my trust? Since I know he's been dishonest before, I will have to continue monitoring his behavior and words diligently to make sure he doesn't do it again. For me and my business (sadly), it's not worth it. My business is not a rehabilitation center, but a business that employs honest employees.

Guidelines for Firing – Difficult as it is, these guidelines should help the process go a little smoother.

1. *Fire In Person* – Never fire someone indirectly. Never by text or email, or even phone. Always do it in person. For one thing, it's more respectful of the person if you're standing right there in front of them. Also, people are less likely to lose their cool if you're face to face. Also, if you need to get anything from the employee, like equipment or supplies that are your property, you need to be right there with them.

2. *State Clearly the Reason for the Firing* – He must know why he's being fired. This is your only available attempt to help him get another job in the future. If he knows why he's being fired, he'll know he needs to correct that behavior for his next job. Also, this needs to be clearly stated for your business's legal safety.

3. *Settle any Practical Issues Immediately* – If the employee has equipment or supplies he needs to return, get it immediately or as soon as possible. Check the equipment returned against the document he signed when he was first employed to make sure all is accounted for (see *Equipment List*, p. 142). If the employee still has a partial check (or checks) coming,  withhold the check until all equipment is returned. Ask if he'd like the check mailed to him, deposited directly, or to pick it up as usual.

4. *Remember to Document the Firing* – Write down everything that happens in the firing process; dates, times, locations, and the specific incident that prompted the firing. Document it clearly. You never know when this may be needed in the future.

Firing Examples from My Business

Poaching Clients – I received a call from an elderly client who lives in a retirement complex. She said after my employee finished his work, he gave her several business cards to give to her friends in the complex. She thought it was odd when she noticed the phone number on the cards was not the same she had called to arrange the service. I went to see her in person, and she gave me the cards he had left. They were for a different auto detailing company and the phone number was his own cell phone. She said she'd also seen him putting cards on the windshields of cars in the parking lot. I thanked her and left.

I called my employee and told him I needed to meet with him that same day. We met at McDonald's (a public place is best) and I slid one of his business cards across the table and asked him to explain it. He hung his head and admitted that he was trying to open his own detailing business.

I really liked the guy and at first wanted to give him another chance. But after thinking about it overnight, I changed my mind and decided to fire him. If I'd kept him on as an employee, I would always be suspecting that he was gathering up my clients for himself on the side. Instead of having an employee I couldn't trust wholeheartedly, I decided to fire him and replace him with someone I could trust.

Lying to Me – A client called the business phone and said my employee was still on site and had not completed the detailing job. He had told her it was taking a little longer but he was going to call his boss (me) and tell me he was finished. She said she didn't think it was right for him to lie to his boss, so she called me. I decided to drop by the work site. On the way, I received a text from the employee stating he was finished. When I arrived,

I showed him the text on my phone and asked him to explain it to me. He said it had taken longer than usual because he had been on his phone a lot dealing with a family problem.

I explained the gravity of lying to me, and also telling the client he was going to lie to his boss. He needed to understand his action worsened the trust of the client in our business as well. If he was having problems with family, he should take care of the current client, then deal with family issues. It was not fair for the client to be tied up longer than anticipated.

I helped the employee finish the vehicle, but allowed the client to pay whatever she felt it was worth. I apologized for the behavior of my employee, and stressed I wanted her to believe in the integrity of our company. I told the employee I wasn't sure what I was going to do, so we should talk about this again the following morning at 10am.

I had him meet me at my home, and told him I could not have an employee who would lie to me. He needed to return all the equipment and then he would get his last check. He argued, "You're going to fire me over one lie?" I tried to explain that I could not be sure his "one lie" would not be repeated to the point of habitual lying; nor did I know for sure that he'd not lied to me before. This was the first lie I'd found out about—were there more? If I let it go, would he just get more proficient at lying and cover it up better? I could not take the chance.

BUSINESS
The Devil's in the Details!

You are in business to make a profit. You are in business for yourself because you want to have the freedom to make your own decisions which you think will provide an income for you (and your family) for the foreseeable future. So, why would I ask this question which has such an obvious answer? Because the way you answer this "why" question, will help you make "what" decisions in the future.

Let me explain by giving an example from my own car detailing business. The set of equipment and supplies I provide for my employees to use on their jobs costs about $1500 a set. Each set is assigned to a specific detailing tech. Whether the detailer does 12 cars a week or 5 cars a week, he has the same equipment. If I have enough business to offer a detailer 12 cars a week, but he's only got time for 5 cars a week, I'm losing the profit which could come from those 7 undetailed cars.

Since my "why" says the purpose of being in business is to make a profit, I must make some changes. Either I let the employee know he needs to detail more cars, or I need to hire someone who will. This sounds like a threatening ultimatum, but it's actually just a logical conclusion. Remember, my purpose is not just to provide jobs for my employees, but to use every means available to turn a profit.

Knowing why you are in business helps make this decision easy.

WHERE ARE YOU WORKING?

This may sound like another trick question, but here goes. Track with me here: Are you working IN your business or ON your business?

When you are asked the question, "What do you do?" perhaps your answer is something like, "I clean houses" or "I am a window washer." When you are actually doing that activity, you are working IN your business.

You know there are other activities you must complete to make sure you can work in your business. You must receive payment from clients, deposit the money in the bank, and purchase materials for your business. When you complete these activities, you are working ON your business.

> **Working IN your business** – actually doing the work for the client

> **Working ON your business** – all the "behind the scenes" activities

Working IN your business is where the income is generated and the reason you're **B**uilding **Y**our **O**wn **B**usiness to start with. But working ON your business allows all that income to come in! You have to divide your time in such a way that you make sure each of these areas is covered. The material in this book is concerned with working ON your business. If you don't already know how to work IN your business, that is, to perform the specific service your new business will provide, you'll have to seek that information elsewhere.

DANGER #1: Some business owners will spend so much time working ON their business that they don't work IN their business. The consequences will quickly  become obvious: no income! You can't make any money by only working on the budget, marketing, or changing your business Facebook page. While these are important activities, by themselves they won't generate income.

DANGER #2: Some business owners avoid working ON their business so much that soon their business is unmanageable. Undeposited checks and cash are piling up, they're running out of supplies, and clients are complaining because they haven't received their receipts.

IN OR ON: HOW TO BALANCE YOUR TIME

SOLUTION: Assuming you have no employees in the beginning, here's what I propose. You'll have to adjust this as you go along, but in the beginning, set as a goal to spend 1/3 of your work time working ON your business and 2/3 of your time working IN your business. So, if you spend eight hours cleaning houses during the day, spend four hours at night doing those behind the scenes tasks.

DAILY TASKS:
- Compile cash & checks for deposit the next day
- Enter invoices into your records (online or on paper – see p. 33)
- Send receipts to clients (by email or "snail" mail)
- Completing work logs (if you have employees – see *Work Log*, p. 163)

WEEKLY TASKS:
- Check your supplies to see what needs to be purchased or ordered for delivery
- Spend time marketing your business (see *Advertising*, p. 89)
- Payroll preparation (if you have employees, see *Payroll*, p. 159)
- Spend time on a government/taxes task (see *Self-Employment* Tax, p. 84, and *Employee Taxes*, p. 159)

MONTHLY TASKS:
- Keep up to date on government registrations or renewals of your business license, unemployment filings, and other governmental

requirements (perhaps schedule each to a specific week of the month)

- Sales tax reporting with the state or county government
- Evaluate current and possible future marketing ideas and take action to reject or accept them

---

IN or ON: A Real Example Schedule

Monday – Friday
     8am-3pm - working IN your business
     6pm-9pm – working ON your business

Saturday
     8am-12pm – working IN your business
     1pm-3pm – working ON your business

Sunday
     1pm-3pm – working ON your business (setting
            up the schedule for week to come)

As I said before, you'll probably have to adjust this schedule as you go along, but it's a good place to start. If you see some details not being taken care of after a few weeks, adjust your work flow. You'll get to know your own work rhythm in a few months.

IN OR ON: EMPLOYEES OR HIRING OUT?

If you begin to see you have so much work that you can't keep up with it all by yourself, it's time to reach out for help. You can get help either ON your business or IN your business.

ON your Business: Hire employees who will do the work with you or for you (See *Employees I*, p. 132, and *Employees II*, p. 148)

IN your Business: Hire someone to take care of some of the administrative tasks

As mentioned earlier (p. 132), an employee can help in several ways. He can be an assistant to help you on the job by doing all your tasks quicker. He can be the "gofer" who goes back to the truck for more supplies, or picks up the other end of that table you need to move.

With an employee, you can move through clients at a quicker pace. Or, you can train the employee to do what you do, or at least prepare a job for you to finish. You can send him ahead to get everything ready  for you to begin work immediately upon arrival, saving you time, and making you money!

IN your business, you may want to hire a bookkeeper part-time to keep up with your finances, receipts, payroll, and taxes. Perhaps you'll find a marketer who will do all the advertising for your business.

"But I can't' afford that!" Think of it this way: Those ON your business tasks must be done, right? If there aren't enough hours in a day to do them, you'll have to take away time from clients to make sure the tasks get done. If you make $50 an hour working IN your business, wouldn't it be worth it to pay someone $20 an hour to take those tasks off your plate? Instead of losing $50/hr by not working for income, you're only "losing" $20 to see those tasks completed. For those hours, you're actually making $30 an hour!

SEASONAL SLUMPS IN BUSINESS

Depending on the business you choose, you may have a cyclical slump in business every year at the same time of year. If you have a lawn care business, you will certainly cut more grass in the summer months. So, what do you do during the slower winter period?

Be sure your employees know about the seasonal nature of your business. When you hire on for the "high season," be sure they know things may drop off during the "low season." If your high season is in the summer (like our detailing business), your summer staff may be partly made up of college students who will be going back to school in the fall. This will help you not have to lay them off when the cycle slows down.

Prepare financially for the slower months. During the high season, sock away some savings to help out with regular "non-cyclical" expenses during the down months.

Try to arrange for many of the month-to-month expenses to be taken care of in the high months. Some month-to-month subscriptions or other types of expenses, such as advertising, may be able to be paid in full when the income is high.

Realize (and repeat to yourself daily) that the down cycle is always followed by the up cycle! Don't allow yourself to be troubled when this happens year after year. As the saying goes, "What goes up, must come down"—wait, reverse that!

BIG PROPOSALS

Occasionally, you'll be asked to do a larger than normal job for which you will have to do some extra planning. Perhaps in your window washing business, your regular client is a homeowner, but a school calls and wants you to give them a bid for doing all the windows in the school during the summer months. What extra items should you consider?

How many "man hours" will it take to complete the job? If you normally work by yourself, you'd just determine how many hours it would take you to do the job. If you need help, add all the worked hours together to determine the "man hours" needed. For example, if it will take 3 of you 8 hours per day for 2 days to complete the job, it will take 48 man hours (3x8x2=48).

How much will you pay yourself (and any help you hire) per hour? Perhaps you could hire some helpers who don't know all the ins and outs of your service, but they can help you get things done quicker. You may pay them a fair but lower wage for this short-term commitment.

How much in materials will be used to do the job? How much extra soap or other cleaning supplies do you need to purchase ahead of time?

What extra equipment may be needed (or expedient to use) for this large job? Are there any special brushes or longer poles that you will need for this job? Is renting a lift for this big two-day job a good use of your money?

Your margin of profit needs to be worth the extra effort and the time away from other clients. Once you've determined how much it would cost you to perform this special service, you're still not finished determining the bid price. If you were *not* doing this job for these two days, how much would you have expected to make working for your regular clients? How much profit will make you glad you went to the trouble and headache of doing something out of the ordinary for this job?

Labor (48hrs x $12/hr)	575	
Materials	250	
Equipment Rental	<u>375</u>	
Total COST	1200	
(if you made this, you'd break even)		

Normal Income ($250/day)	500
(what you'd normally be making without this job)	

Bonus for extra trouble	<u>500</u>
Total BID PRICE	$2200
(what you will happily do the job for)	

Sometimes you may have to bargain for the job, but not often. Honestly, I've rarely had to haggle over the price. They either accept it or not, and I'm fine with that. If you feel you need some negotiation room, bid higher so you can come down to your "real" price. But this higher than needed bid may knock you out of the running for the job. It's your call.

Prepare a written proposal for clarity and professionalism. I like preparing a proposal because then I know exactly what I'm offering for a specific amount of money. Also, the potential client will have this professional document to present to her authorities for approval. For additional help with it, examine my *Example Proposal* on page 192.

Your business could take advantage of the use of gift certificates for family or friends to buy for their loved ones. There are definite advantages but a few disadvantages to consider.

A gift certificate allows you to have the money now for a job yet to be competed. This allows you to spend it on current expenses when you don't have to provide the labor until later. Especially if you're selling the gift certificates in the low season, these sales are very helpful.

Realize you owe a debt of service which will be required in the future. Once the gift certificate is given, it can be redeemed at any time (unless you've stipulated something different in the agreement). When the work is done to honor this certificate, there will be no income to accompany the work. You will have to work those hours without being paid for them (because you've *already been paid*). Many times, if the gift certificate was purchased during the low season, it will be redeemed in the high season. This works well for your business, because although you will not be paid for the gift certificate hours, there is enough work before and after to make up the difference.

You must have a way to deliver the gift certificate to the purchaser (or the recipient). Our business does all of this by email. We have a digital gift certificate (a PDF document) which can be attached to an email and sent to the purchaser. He can then print it out or even forward the email itself to the recipient.

Be sure to include all the pertinent details on the gift certificate. It should have your business information (name and/or logo, contact info), the type of service purchased or dollar amount to credit, and the date of expiration for the certificate.

Your options for a gift certificate are numerous. It could be a completely paid for service where the bearer only schedules the service and pays nothing (*Free Premium Detail for your Minivan!*). You could offer a dollar amount applied to any service you offer (*$200 Off Your Next Lawn Service!*).

What to do about tipping? Normally, tips are not included in gift certificates. If your service business lends itself to tipping, be sure to delicately indicate this to the recipient. I usually say something like, "While tipping is certainly not required, please understand that no tip was included in the purchase of the gift certificate."

Daily Tasks

To have a successful business, you must complete some very specific daily tasks. I can tell you from experience that you do not want to get behind on these very simple tasks. If you do them every day, without exception, your life will be easier. If you miss a day, you won't die, but you'll be very sad you didn't take my advice and do them every day!

There are just four tasks—two looking forward, and two looking backward.

1. Setting Appointments

You must have a system for answering requests from potential clients. Answering the phone, email, and website requests must be a priority. Your 1-, 5-, and 10-minute pitches will come in handy here if you have them down by memory (see *Pitching Your Business*, p. 36). Setting appointments with former and new clients is the lifeblood of your business. If this doesn't happen, you will not have to worry about anything else in your business!

As you set appointments, you'll need to make sure you estimate time needed to complete the task, travel time between home and clients, and travel between clients if you or your employees do more than one per day.

Helpful Hint: You may want to give a time range for your arrival time. If you're traveling to a client's home, you will want to account for the unknown traffic factor and other unforeseen delays. In our business, we give ourselves a 30-minute buffer. I try to make light of it with the client by saying something like, "At least we don't make you wait four hours like the cable guy!"

2. Assigning Appointments

If you have employees, you'll need to assign each appointment to an employee. If they are traveling to an appointment, you'll want to keep several factors in mind. Here's what I think of for my business:

- **The location of the client** in reference to where the detailer lives – if a client lives in the same neighborhood as one of my detailers, this employee will most likely get the assignment.
- **The distance between clients** in one given day – if two clients are in the same general area, the same detailer will most likely be assigned both clients.
- **The time needed** to complete a job – if a detailer has a harder job in the morning, I will try to assign a lighter job in the afternoon, rather than give two hard jobs to one detailer.

3. Updating Work Log

At the end of the day, make sure to place accurate information in the work log (p. 163). You want to make sure this information is kept up to date. If it's not, you'll have to talk with each employee and ask them to remember what happened days in the past. The information will not be as accurate and any problems which happened with a client may not be reported soon enough for you to rectify them.

Added bonus: If you've been communicating with your employees daily by text or email, this practice provides another layer of information to reference when trying to reconstruct the week's assignments for the work log.

4. Updating Financial Records

Just like the work log update mentioned above, the financial records must be kept up to date. Trying to figure out after the fact what happened in an appointment, or whether the client paid by check, cash, or credit card is increasingly difficult the farther back you have to remember.

Keeping these four activities on your daily To Do List will save you tons of headaches in your business. Why put off what will take only a few minutes, when you know it will take much more effort later? *Do them every day!*

One characteristic that sets successful businesses apart from businesses that fail is learning how to change quickly when the need arises. We don't live in a stagnant world; it is constantly changing. We must adapt to change or we'll go the way of the dinosaur, and find ourselves in an environment where we can't survive anymore!

Suppose someone calls you one day and asks if you can help them with a certain issue you've never dealt with before? Instead of saying, "No ma'am, we don't handle that," say something like, "Could you give me some time to think that through and email you a proposal?"

NOTE: In my detailing business, I get calls each year for several of the car shows in Nashville. I wasn't sure what to do when they first started calling. I had to ask a lot of questions at first. But after the first few shows, I learned how I could benefit my clients, and what would make sense for the business financially. I would send a proposal to them. This served to give them assurance that I was a professional, but also, it gave me time to think through costs and a proposed fee without feeling the pressure to determine all this while on the phone with them.

(See *Example Proposal*, p. 192).

For example, suppose one day you receive a call from a potential client asking about your window washing service. She says she and her neighbor want go in together to get the windows on their houses done the same day. She asks if she could have a discount for such an arrangement. What will you do? Tell them you're very interested, and would like to send them a proposal in the afternoon. You may see that since you don't have to travel far between jobs, you can give them a 5-10% discount! You determine what would help you and them, then put it in the proposal. You win, and they feel they've won too!

Don't turn down an opportunity to do something new with your business. It could turn into something very profitable for you and beneficial for your clients!

EXAMPLE PROPOSAL:

June 10, 2017

TO: Mr. Joe Example
FROM: Steve Young, RENEW Mobile Detailing
RE: Proposal for Cleaning Show Trailers – Nice Show Trailers, Inc.

CONTACT INFORMATION:
Steve Young, owner
3260 My Address Street
Nashville TN 00000
RENEW Mobile Detailing
contact@renewdetailing.com
555-555-5555

PROPOSAL DETAILS:
- RENEW will provide on-site detailing services for 10 show trailers on site at the Music City Center on August 8, 2017 beginning at 830am.
- The on-site detailing shall include wipe down of all exterior surfaces of trailers with wash and microfiber towels, spot treating any areas for bugs or grease stains, cleaning the wheels, and shining the tires. All will be performed with minimal drip off in the area.
- RENEW shall supply their own supplies & water. No machines will be used in the process, so no electrical generators will be used (as it is prohibited in the Music City space).

BID DETAILS:
- Nice Show will provide authorized access to the building for Renew detailers and their equipment.
- RENEW agrees to faithfully complete these activities in a timely fashion for $660.
- Payment shall be received within 5 business days of completed job (preferably the day of the job). Major credit cards or checks are accepted.

*B*uilding *Y*our *O*wn *B*usiness *In 30 Days!*
Checklist

WEEK ONE: FOUNDATION PHASE

- ☐ Determine the service your business will provide. (p. 14)
- ☐ Check out competing services in your area. (p. 15)
- ☐ Write out the foundational values you will have for your business. (p. 17)
- ☐ Decide on the name for your business. (p. 22)
- ☐ Determine your scope of services—what is included or not. (p. 23)
- ☐ Design your perfect client, or your "avatar." (p. 25)
- ☐ Determine the prices you will charge for each service. (p. 26)

WEEK TWO: SETUP PHASE

- ☐ List the basic materials you need to begin – tools & supplies. (p. 31)
- ☐ Buy the tools & supplies you are lacking. (p. 32)

- [ ] Decide on an accounting system for your business (paper or online), purchase it, and enter all expenses thus far. (p. 33)
- [ ] Set up business phone number and business email account. (p. 34)
- [ ] Design "pitch scripts" in 1-minute, 5-minutes, and 10-minute formats. (p. 36)
- [ ] Design phone "script" for answering and/or returning calls. (p. 37)

WEEK THREE: BUSINESS PHASE

- [ ] Get your business license and Federal Employer Identification Number (FEIN). (p. 41)
- [ ] Set up government accounts with your state or county – Sales Tax, Labor, etc. (p. 44)
- [ ] Open a business bank account, or accounts. (p. 46)
- [ ] Set up account with credit card processor, if accepting credit/debit cards. (p. 48)
- [ ] Set up Facebook account for your business and other free online locations. (p. 51)
- [ ] Print business cards. (p. 52)
- [ ] Get insurance for your business (recommended, but optional). (p. 55)

Week Four: MARKETING PHASE

☐ Begin "spreading the word" about your new business at least one week before beginning to accept clients. (p. 59)

☐ Do some "freebies" or deeply discounted services for friends & family for reviews or references. (p. 59)

☐ Attend local networking meetings to tell about your new business. (p. 60)

☐ Purchase the website domain for your business. (p. 60)

☐ Set up a simple website. (p. 62)

NOTES:

INDEX

Abundance Attitude....21, 66

Account, Business Savings......................81

Accountant 44, 78, 84, 86

Accounting............ 33, 78

Accounting System...... 33

Advances in Payment for Employees............. 160

Advertise for Employees 134

Advertising...... 63, 89, 98

All-Up-In-Your-Business Clients...................... 113

American Express..49, 51

Angie's List............ 52, 90

Angry Clients.............153

Apologize to Employees 149

Appointments, Assigning 187

Appointments, Setting 186

Arrival Time..............186

Assignments for Employees.......149, 151

Attitude........................ 66

Attitude, Abundance....21

Authority with Employees..............136

Auto-Payment Credit Cards........... 115

Avatar................ 25, 108

Aweber Email............ 101

B2B, Business To Business.................. 101

Background Check....135, 140, 154

Back-To-School........... 94

Bank Account, Business 46, 87

Bank Account, Personal 47

Bathroom Wall Ads for Marketing.............. 96

Benefits to Client. 93, 108

Better Business Bureau, BBB..............52, 80, 90

Business Cards...... 52, 92

Business to Business, B2B..........................101

Buyer Beware............. 96

BYOBin30days.com..... 3, 48, 69, 96

Calendars, Promotional Marketing.............. 95

Capital, Business.........19

Cash........................ 120

Categories, Financial ..81

Caveat Emptor........... 96

Checklist, Business......10, 194

Checks from Clients.... 49

Clarification with Clients 117

Clients .25, 68, 73, 90, 91, 105, 148

Common Sense 110

Communication with Employees 150

Competition, Competitors.15, 20, 68, 89, 92, 128

Complaints from Clients 76, 117

Computer, Home 50

Confidence of Clients 106, 153

Contracts, Long-Term .19

Convenience to Clients 107

Conversation with Employees 152

Cooperate with Competitors............129

Correction of Employees ..142, 151, 152, 164, 167

Coupons 95, 101

Craigslist......................91

Credit Card Processor 48, 50

Credit Cards.. 19, 115, 120

Culture, Company 145

Customers or Clients .105

Danger to Employees 155

DBA, "Doing Business As" 23, 41, 47

Debt..............................18

Deliver, Over- for Clients 112

Department Of Labor . 45

Department Of Revenue 45

Deposit Required from Clients..................... 119

Difficult Clients 113

Direct Deposit 141

Discipline of Employees 151, 166

Discounts 94, 96, 100, 116, 119

Discounts for Marketing 59

Discover Card........49, 51

Dishonesty of Employees 167

DOCUMENTATION with Employees 164, 170

Domain, Website . 35, 60, 100

Draw, Owner's 86

Email List Of Clients. 100

Email, Business.....34, 61, 100, 117

Emails to Employees .152

*EMPLOYEES*68, 132, 148

Equipment ....See Tools & Equipment

Equipment, Future 81

Expectations of Employees 146

Expectations for an Employee................138

Expectations Of The Client 121

Expectations, Unclear Or Unmet....................139

EXPENSES....... 47, 79, 81

Expenses, Tax Deductible *84*
Extensions, Website *61*
F.A.T., Faithful, Available, Teachable *137, 164*
Facebook *12, 51, 75, 89, 90, 91, 98, 135, 176, 195*
Facebook, Business Acccount *51*
Fairness *149*
Father's Day *94*
Features of Services *94*
FEIN, Federal Employer Idendification Number *41, 43*
Finances *149*
Financial Categories ... *81*
Financial Records *188*
Finding Employees *134*
Firing Employees *166*
Firing Clients *114*
Firing Guidelines of Employees *169*
First Clients *73*
First Impressions of Clients *152*
First Impressions of Candidate *137*
Fiverr.Com *53*
Freebies For Marketing *59*
Gift Certificates *184*
Giveaways for Marketing *90*
Godaddy.Com *62, 100*
Google *52*

Google Business ... *90, 99, 129*
Government ... *44, 84, 126*
Gross Income *82*
Guidelines for Firing Employees *169*
High Season *133*
Hiring Employes *132, 133, 178*
Holidays *94*
Homestead Exemption *86*
Honesty *17, 67, 167*
I-9 Form *140*
Inappropriate Domain Name *62*
INCOME *47, 79, 81*
Incorporated, Inc. *22*
Instagram *89, 99*
Insurance, Business *55*
Integrity *67*
Interaction with Clients by Employees *137*
Interaction with Clients by Employees *152*
INTERNET *63, 98, 125*
Interview by Phone ... *136*
Interview Candidate .. *137*
Invoicing Clients 116, 120
IRS.Gov *43*
Labor Office of the State *166*
Latin *96*
Lawsuits from Employees *160*
Learning, On-Going .. *189*
Ledger, Accounting *33*
License, Business ... *41, 42*

Link for Client Payment 50, 121

Listen to Clients ... 38, 76, 117

LLC, Limited Liability Company 41, 42

Logo For Business 53

Lying from Employees 140, 171

Mailchimp 101

Maintenance of Tools & Equipment 124

Man Hours 181

Managing Employees 148

Marketing 24, 53, 59, 89, 93, 95

Mastercard 49, 51

Michalowicz, Mike 47

Mobile Friendly Website 63

MONEY 27, 78

Monthly Clients 115

Mother's Day 94

Name, Business 22, 41, 47, 60, 62

National-Day-Of Events 95

Net Income 81

Networking in Business 60, 89

No Go Client 113

Non-Compete Contract 141

Non-Payment of Clients 120

Oceans, Blue & Red 128

Online 91, 98

Online Marketing 51

Owner's Draw 47, 86

Pain Points of Clients. 94, 108, 116

Paying Employees 155

Payment from Clients 110, 119

Payment Schedule for Employees 157

Paypal 50

Payroll Account 159

Payroll Company 159

Phone Calls to Employees 151

Phone Script 37

Phone, Business 34, 90

Pinterest 99

Pitch Script 36, 60

Pitches, Business. 90, 186

Poaching Clients by Employees 171

Prices 26, 92

Prices, Raising 27

Professional Appearance 92, 152

Professionalism 109, 129, 183

PROFIT ... 47, 68, 79, 174, 182

Profit & Loss Statement, P&L 82, 85

Profit First Book 47

Project615.Org 146

Promise, Under- to Clients 112

Property Taxes 86

Proposal, Written

for Clients...... 101, 122, 183, 189, 190, 192
Proposals for Business 181
Protection of Employees 153
Puns For Business Name 22, 62
Purpose Of Business ..174
Quarterly Taxes.......... 84
Quickbooks......33, 87, 117
Radio Ads..................... 95
Reasons For Firing Employees 167
Receipt for Clients 116
Recurring Charges for Clients...................... 82
Recurring Charges for the Business............. 83
References................... 59
Referrals 60, 75
Repairing Tools & Equipment..............125
Repetition in Training 143
ReplacingTools & Equipment..............125
Research, Market 66
Respect for Employees 137, 148
Respectful Employees 136
Restaurant Table-Top Ads for Marketing... 96
Resume.......................135
Reviews from Clients. 59, 99, 102
Reward For Self...........57
Safe Guards 110

Sales...........................81
Sales Tax..................... 44
Sandwich Of Correction for Employees 165
Satisfaction of Clients 122
Scarcity, The Principle of 111
Schedule for Business 178
School Sponsorships... 95
Scope Of Services 23, 118, 122, 153
Script...........................37
Seasonal Promotions.. 94
Seasons in Business .. 180
Secret Weapon of Marketing 111
Secretary Of State 43
Security for Employees 133
Self-Employment Taxes 84
Service to Clients 106, 112
Service Business 8, 14
Share with Competitors 129
Sick Leave for Employees 162
Slumps in Business ... 180
Social Media Marketing 99, 100
Sole Proprietorship..... 40
Specials 94, 100
Square™ 50
Staples Office Supply.. 55
Storage of Tools & Equipment..............124
Strengths in Business 129
Sue, Lawsuits............ 160

Supplies
    Tools & Equipment .. 5,
        33, 81, 87
Supplies, Replenishable
    32
System, Financial 87
Talkative Clients 113
TASKS for Business .. 177,
    185
Tax Deductible Expenses
    84
Text For Payment 121
Texting Employees 151
Texting Tip For
    Interviewing
    Employees 138
Theft by Employees ...154
Theft, Accusation 154
Third Party Paying ...110
Time 133, 148, 151, 187
Time Off for Employees
    161
Time, Balancing.........176
Time, Business 27
Time, Punctuality 112
Time, Wasting 100
Tips 81, 121, 185
Tools & Equipment 32,
    80, 87, 124, 142, 182
Training Employees ..142
Travel Payment 156
Trust

Clients 107, 109
    Employees 169
Twitter 99
Types Of Businesses.... 40
Unemployment
    Insurance 45
Unequal.....................150
Unfair 150
Values, Business 17
Visa 49, 51
W-4 Form................. 140
W-9 Form.................. 101
Warranty
    Tools & Equipment 124
Weaknesses,
    Business..................129
Website..... 23, 35, 54, 62,
    63, 90, 100
WII-FM, What's In It For
    Me? 93
Wordpress 63
Work History 135
Work Logs...149, 163, 187
Working IN Your
    Business.................. 175
Working ON Your
    Business.................. 175
Workman's Comp 159
Yelp 16, 52, 89, 91, 99,
    129
Youtube 63, 125

Made in the USA
Monee, IL
05 November 2021